UNIVERSITY OF NEW MEXICO PUBLICATIONS
IN BIOLOGY

NUMBER SIX

THE FERNS AND FERN ALLIES
OF NEW MEXICO

Howard J. Dittmer

Edward F. Castetter

Ora M. Clark

Drawings by Jeanne R. Janish

THE UNIVERSITY OF NEW MEXICO PRESS
ALBUQUERQUE : 1954

UNIVERSITY OF NEW MEXICO PUBLICATIONS
JOHN N. DURRIE
General Editor

PUBLICATIONS IN BIOLOGY
EDWARD F. CASTETTER
Editor

A PATHFINDER BOOK REPRINT EDITION
Complete and Unabridged

Printed in the United States of America

ISBN: 979-8869056733

PREFACE

One might well express marked surprise at seeing a manual such as this on the ferns of New Mexico since, in the minds of most people, the state is definitely regarded as a hot and dry country—anything but a "fern state." However, a little reflection, or at least investigation, will reveal two interesting and important facts regarding the fern flora of the state: (1) Although New Mexico has wide stretches of flat, desertlike country, it is also characterized by numerous mountains. Despite the fact that some of these are small, desert mountains, there are also to be found massive, wooded mountain ranges, and parts of these are fully as productive of ferns as are many of the mountains of the eastern United States. Thus, the bracken fern, which may attain a height of 4 feet, is a very conspicuous plant in certain of our mountain areas, often forming a dense undergrowth beneath stands of Douglas fir, aspen, spruce, or yellow pine. Interesting examples are to be found in the Santa Fe and Las Vegas mountains in the Sangre de Cristo Range and in the western part of the Mogollon Mountains, where the bracken covers entire hillsides; nearly comparable abundance is to be seen in places with the Fragile or Bladder Fern and certain species of *Woodsia*. (2) The arid regions of the state support numerous species of relatively small ferns which grow and thrive in unbelievably warm and dry situations and persist year after year in their desert habitat. These "desert" ferns grow very slowly, making their growth during short, moist periods, then curling up and remaining practically dormant during unfavorable periods. Many of these resume active growth even during moist periods in winter. These ferns are very hardy and are often found in crevices of shaded, rocky cliffs or in some cases in cracks of rock "pavement" in wide-open areas with no protecting vegetation.

That ferns are common in New Mexico is to be seen from the fact that this manual lists 7 families, 24 genera, and 75 species and varieties of ferns and fern allies, although several of these have not yet been found in the state. By comparison, Harrington and Durrell[1] listed 22 genera and 63 species and

---

[1] *Colorado Ferns*, Fort Collins, 1950.

varieties (or subspecies) for Colorado; Lyness,[2] 56 species and varieties for Iowa; and Flowers,[3] 20 genera and 53 species for Utah.

Many of the New Mexican species are represented by small, inconspicuous plants. A few are rare, having been reported only once or a very few times for the state. Several species have never been reported as collected from the state, but they are listed here because of the fact that their known general distribution suggests that they do occur in New Mexico. Moreover, it is hoped that listing and figuring them in the manual will encourage botanists and laymen to search for them. For these missing species the descriptions and drawings were based on specimens collected in areas adjacent to New Mexico.

Following is a list of ferns and fern allies described in the text which have not yet been verified by specimens as occurring within the state. However, the fact that they do occur in terrain of contiguous states quite similar to that of areas in New Mexico strongly suggests that they will be found within the borders of the state.

1. **Polystichum Lonchitis** (L.) Roth ex Roem.
2. **Notholaena Grayii** Davenp.
3. **Notholaena Aschenborniana** Klotzsch.
4. **Cryptogramma Stelleri** (Gmel.) Prantl.
5. **Polypodium thyssanolepis** A. Br. ex Klotzsch.
6. **Botrychium multifidum** ssp. **Coulteri** (Underw.) Clausen.
7. **Botrychium lanceolatum** (Gmel.) Angstr., ssp. **typicum** Clausen.
8. **Botrychium Lunaria** (L.) Swartz.
9. **Ophioglossum Engelmannii** Prantl.
10. **Isoëtes Bolanderi** Engelm.
11. **Selaginella arizonica** Maxon.

Tidestrom and Kittell[4] report the following species, either definitely or by inference, as occurring in New Mexico. How-

---

[2] Amer. Fern Journ. 23: 34-49. 1933.

[3] Bull. Univ. Utah v. 35, Biol. Ser. v. 4, no. 6. 1944.

[4] *A Flora of Arizona and New Mexico*, Washington, pp. 862-881. 1941.

ever, since they have not yet been verified by herbarium specimens either in New Mexico or in contiguous states, they are not included or described in this manual.

1. **Osmunda cinnamomea** L., Sp. Pl. 1066. 1753.

This species has been reported definitely as occurring in New Mexico. The record could be valid but we have located no herbarium specimen to support it.

2. **Notholaena candida** (Mart. and Gal.) Hook., Sp. Fil. 5: 110. 1864.

This species was definitely reported as growing in the state. The record is doubtful, however, and more likely refers to *N. Copelandii* C. C. Hall.[5] Mrs. Hall knew it only from Texas and Mexico.

3. **Adiantum Jordanii** C. Mühl, Bot. Zeit. 1864.

This report of definite occurrence in western New Mexico is probably erroneous since, so far as known, the species is confined to Oregon and California.

4. By inference New Mexico is included in the range of *Pteridium latiusculum* (Desv.) Hieron. ex R. E. Fries, Wiss. Ergebn. Schwed. Rhod.-Kongo-Exp. 1: 7. 1914, now commonly called *P. aquilinum* var. *latiusculum* (Desv.) Underw. This record probably involves a misidentification and doubtless should have been *P. aquilinum* var. *pubescens* Underw., which is the variety found in the West, var. *latiusculum* being generally regarded as a purely Eastern plant. However, Harrington and Durrell[6] list var. *latiusculum* as occurring in Colorado.

5. **Botrychium virginianum** (L.) Swartz, Journ. Bot. Schrad. 1800 (2): 111. 1801.

Although reported by inference as occurring within the state, this inclusion may have been only a supposition; it is possible, however, that the species is to be found within the state.

---

[5] Amer. Fern Journ. 40: 178-187. 1950.
[6] *Colorado Ferns,* Fort Collins, p. 47. 1950.

6. Marsilea macropoda Engelm. ex A. Br., Amer. Journ. Sci. II 3: 56. 1847 was reported as occurring in New Mexico. This reference doubtless was based on Wright's Collection No. 2111, a specimen of which is in the United States National Herbarium marked as from New Mexico without further locality. There is another specimen under the same number in the Gray Herbarium of Harvard University. At our request Dr. Robert C. Foster[7] has carefully examined this sheet as well as the circumstances surrounding the collection of the plant and is positive that the specimen was collected not in New Mexico but in Texas. Moreover, C. S. Correll,[8] in his preliminary survey of the Texas Pteridophyta, stated that the species is apparently confined to southern Texas.

This manual has been written primarily for the use of the serious layman student of ferns and for the botanist. Although the general reader will also find the treatise useful, he will find it somewhat difficult to identify certain of the species without serious and consistent application. In the interest of accuracy, technical descriptive terms have been used freely throughout the manual and, although these will usually be unfamiliar to him, the layman is encouraged to make use of the extensive glossary which has been prepared. The figures have been prepared with painstaking care, particular attention being given to definitive detail which will be of assistance in making generic and specific determinations. Nevertheless, the student will usually be unsuccessful in his efforts to identify a given fern by attempting to match a plant with one of the drawings. It is important that he also make use of the keys and descriptions.

In order further to assist the student in identifying species, a conventionalized labeled diagram (Figure 1) has been prepared for the purpose of graphically illustrating some of the terms and concepts frequently used in the text.

The authors have had substantial assistance from several persons in the preparation of this treatise, and it is a pleasure for us to acknowledge this aid. Especially are we deeply indebted

---

[7] Personal correspondence, September 11, 1953.

[8] Wrightia 1: 269. 1949.

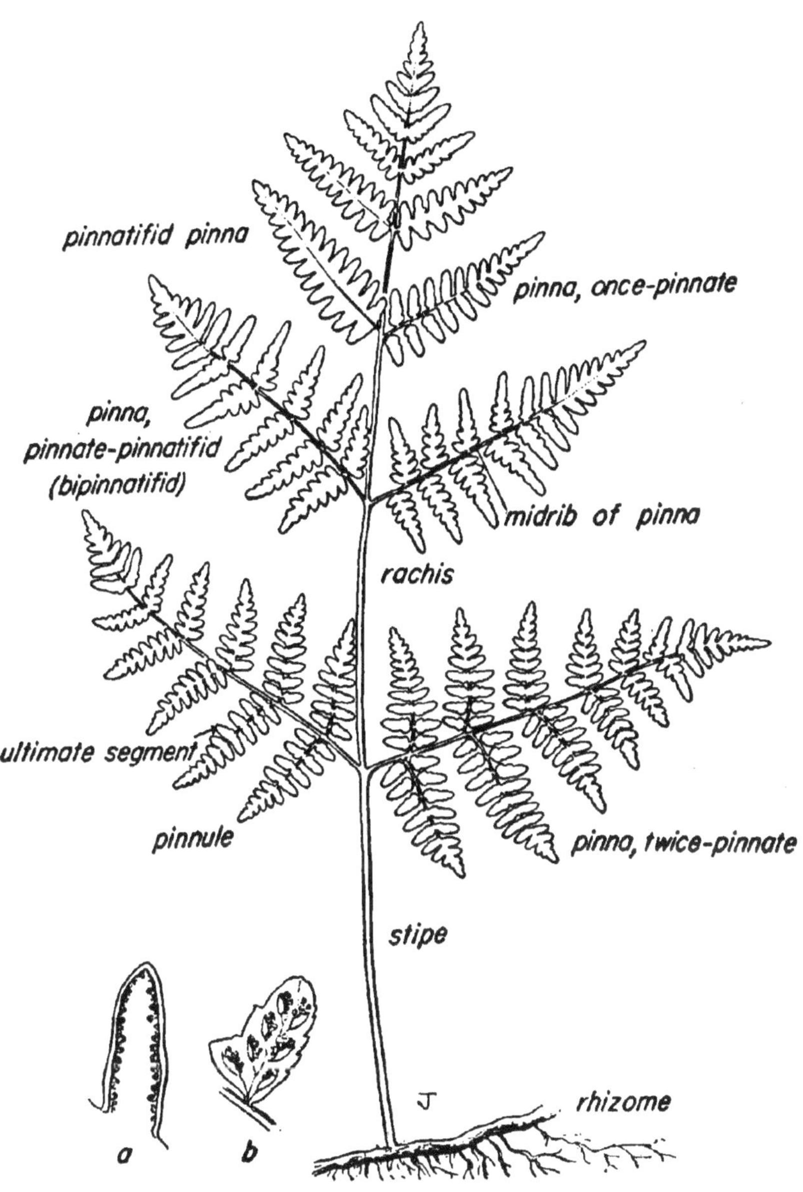

FIGURE 1. Conventionalized diagram of a fern plant. An examination of the right half of the diagram shows the blade to be thrice-pinnate: (a) pinnule showing marginal sori, partly covered by false indusium, (b) pinnule showing sori with true indusia.

to Dr. C. V. Morton, Curator, Division of Ferns, United States National Herbarium, Washington, D. C., for generous and sympathetic cooperation in various ways—for the loan of all New Mexican specimens of ferns in the National Herbarium, for a continuous interest in the manual from its very inception, and for frequent advice and assistance in the preparation of this manuscript. Dr. Rolla M. Tryon, Jr., of the Missouri Botanical Garden, has kindly loaned and made gifts of herbarium specimens and also has critically read and given suggestions on the manuscript, particularly the section on the family Selaginellaceae. We owe special thanks to Miss Katherine G. Simons, Associate Professor of English and Administrative Assistant in the Graduate School at the University of New Mexico, for a careful reading of the manuscript.

To Dr. W. A. Dayton, Chief, Division of Dendrology and Range Forage Investigations of the United States Forest Service, we owe a sincere debt of gratitude for the loan of all New Mexican specimens of Pteridophyta in the United States Forest Service Herbarium at Washington, D. C. To Dr. David B. Dunn, Director of the Herbarium and Assistant Professor of Biology at New Mexico Agricultural and Mechanical College; to Dr. H. D. Harrington, Associate Botanist and Curator of the Herbarium, Colorado Agricultural and Mechanical College; to Dr. W. A. Weber, Assistant Professor of Biology, University of Colorado; and to Dr. George J. Goodman, Professor of Plant Sciences, University of Oklahoma, we are greatly indebted for the loan and gift of herbarium specimens of Pteridophyta.

Finally, we owe sincere thanks to the Committee on Research of the University of New Mexico for continuous financial assistance in support of field work related to this investigation and in the preparation of drawings for the manual.

It is deeply regretted that Mr. Clark's untimely death on December 29, 1952, deprived the other two authors of the benefit of his wise counsel and wide experience in the completion of the manuscript for this manual.

Edward F. Castetter
Howard J. Dittmer

Albuquerque, N. M.
December 1, 1953

CONTENTS

THE FERNS AND FERN ALLIES
OF NEW MEXICO

THE PLANT KINGDOM

The plant kingdom is generally divided into four major divisions based chiefly on organs of reproduction and complexity of tissues. Of these four, the Thallophyta include the bacteria, fungi, and algae and are by far the most heterogeneous of the four groups. The Bryophyta, like the Thallophyta, lack vascular tissue, but the sex organs are contained in a sterile jacket of cells. This group includes the first land plants—the liverworts and mosses. The Pteridophyta, which include plants of much greater complexity than either of the first two groups, have roots, stems, and leaves, a dominant sporophyte, a vascular system, and most of the morphological structures necessary for successful life on land. Although the members of the Pteridophyta for the most part still require water for transfer of sperms to the egg and still have an independent gametophyte, the biggest step in the evolution of plants has been taken with the development of this group. The Spermatophyta, which include the gymnosperms (pines and related plants) and the angiosperms (all flowering plants), no longer require water for fertilization and in addition have made important advances in internal anatomy. The most important advance which this group has made over the Pteridophyta consists in the development of the seed, which first appears as an exposed structure in the cone of the gymnosperms and then is borne enclosed in the ovary (fruit) of the angiosperms. Since this manual is a treatment of the Pteridophyta, no further discussion will be presented on the other three divisions. Additional material on the development of the ferns and their allies follows.

PTERIDOPHYTA

Ferns and their allies have been given the large group name Pteridophyta because of the often feathery appearance of the large leaves (*pteris* = fern; *phyta* = plant). The derivation of the original Greek *pteris* is presumed to be *pteron* (feather). They are characterized as plants having roots, stems, and leaves, but lacking flowers, fruits, and seeds as found in the highest division of the plant kingdom, the seed plants or Spermatophyta. Their internal anatomy is much like that of the higher plants in that they have both *xylem* and *phloem*. Some ferns increase the diameter of their *rhizomes* and aerial stems by means of the activity of an *intercalary meristem*.

Pteridophyta have what is known to the botanist as an *alternation of generations*, in which the large fern plant with which almost everyone is familiar alternates in its development with a small, inconspicuous green structure. The large fern plant is called a *sporophyte* since it produces spores. Each spore falls upon the ground and germinates into a small flat *thallus*, termed the *gametophyte*, which is only a few millimeters in diameter. This thallus (*prothallium*) produces the sexual structures which in ferns and their allies are called *archegonia* for the female part and *antheridia* for the male. The archegonia produce non-motile eggs and the antheridia usually produce multiciliate sperms.

The small gametophytes of many species of Pteridophyta cannot withstand desiccation and consequently develop from the spores only in well-shaded and moist habitats. Furthermore, water is usually necessary for the transfer of the sperms to the archegonia, where fertilization with the egg is accomplished. However, gametophytes of species of *Pellaea*, at least, can withstand desiccation for several months. In this connection, Mrs. Alice F. Tryon, of the staff of the Missouri Botanical Garden, has informed us that she has proved that they can dry up and later revive; it is probable that most of the desert species of ferns do this. Similarly, Pickett[1] has presented data and references on the persistence of *Pellaea* gametophytes. Also, some

---

[1] Amer. Fern Journ. 21: 49-56. 1931.

species of *Pellaea* are known to be apogamous and probably most species of this genus are so. It is likely that most species of desert ferns are apogamous and thus do not require water for fertilization.

After fertilization, the fertilized egg (*zygote*) produces a small root and a small leaf, which constitute the embryo sporophyte. This young sporophyte, which lacks true seed structures such as stored food and seed coat, is immediately exposed to the elements and must grow unaided by any structures other than the prothallium upon which it initiates development. Soon after the first root and leaf have appeared, other roots and leaves arise. These newly formed leaves are true leaves and have a different appearance from that of the first embryo leaf.

Fern leaves have a very characteristic manner of growth, known to the botanist as *circinate vernation,* or growth by an uncoiling process. The upper part of the leaf is coiled like the scroll of a violin, and as it grows the leaves and leaflets enlarge from the base of this coil. Our small ferns have a very small, coiled apex on their developing leaves, but the large tropical tree ferns with leaves over fifteen feet long uncoil from a leaf apex larger than the scroll of a bass viol. Everyone who has a healthy fern will notice this peculiar manner of growth of the fern leaf if he looks closely at the young, developing leaves down in among the older, fully formed ones.

Doubtless many of our readers have observed numerous small brown spots on the under side of fern leaves. Some people erroneously regard these as being a fungus disease on the plant. Although ferns sometimes do have fungus diseases, these are not common. Usually these small brown spots are reproductive structures known as *sori,* which may be distributed in various patterns over the under surface of the leaf or may be marginal and usually more or less covered by the inrolled margin of the leaf. The function of each sorus is to produce *sporangia,* which in turn develop the spores which are necessary to complete the life cycle of a fern.

When the term Pteridophyta is mentioned, we commonly think of ferns; but related to these plants because of their manner of reproduction, internal anatomy, and structure are a number of plants often called fern allies. Some of these allies, such as *Botrychium* and *Ophioglossum,* resemble the ferns somewhat in general appearance. Others are not fernlike as, for example, *Azolla,* a minute, free-floating water plant, called mosquito fern, which is abundant in New Mexico in our freshwater irrigation ditches and other streams, ponds, and lakes. It is easily recognized by its tiny leaves and especially by its purplish color when it grows in masses covering large areas on the water surface. Another fern ally is *Equisetum,* commonly called scouring rush or horsetail. This genus grows abundantly throughout the state along waterways and occasionally in shallow water. Some of the species are branched, others unbranched. The only leaves formed by the horsetails are very small scalelike structures produced in whorls at the stem joints.

Selaginella is the generic name of the spikemosses, another group of fern allies. Superficially they resemble mosses, but actually their anatomy resembles that of some of the higher Pteridophyta. Their manner of gametophyte development, in which the gametophyte is retained within the spore case even after fertilization, probably places it in a position nearer the seed plants than that occupied by any other member of the Pteridophyta. *Selaginella* grows in many places in the state and, although often regarded as a plant preferring moist habitats, it can be found among rocks on many arid hillsides.

As inconspicuous as any of the fern allies is a small plant that looks more like a tuft of grass than a fern. This is the quillwort *(Isoëtes).* This plant has not yet been found in New Mexico, probably because of its inconspicuous habit of growth; but the fact that it has been found in neighboring states suggests that it must be present here also.

In summary, a characterization of those members of the division Pteridophyta found in New Mexico would be this: herbaceous and terrestrial plants, as well as a few aquatic species, chiefly inhabiting well-shaded areas. The period of most active growth is confined to the rainy season. For the most part, they are plants with conspicuous leaves varying from a few inches to several feet in length (except for *Azolla,* which has leaves less than one inch in diameter) . The stems generally are inconspicuous and grow below ground as horizontal rhizomes. Roots are adventitious in their origin and fibrous in appearance, usually dark brown or black in color. The spores are produced in sporangia, which are usually clustered into sori on the under side of the leaves, and are distributed in various patterns either over the leaf surface or along the incurved margin of the leaf.

FOSSIL PTERIDOPHYTA IN NEW MEXICO[2]

The oldest land-plant of fernlike origin found thus far in New Mexico is a primitive horsetail, *Asterocalamites scrobiculatus*, taken from Early Mississippian rocks from the Kelly limestone of the Magdalena mining district, Socorro County. More numerous and better-known fossils of the Pennsylvanian period include the following: *Lepidodendron clypeatum, L. lucidum, L. Keyesii, L. socorroense, L. Thwaitesii*, and possibly several other species of *Lepidodendron*. During this same period other plants of the Pteridophyta division were also abundant in New Mexico; these include *Neuropteris, Calamites, Sphenophyllum, Callipteris, Odontopteris, Sphenopteris, Trigonocarpus*, and several questionable genera.

Rocks of the Abo formation in the Early Permian have also yielded considerable Pteridophyta material. Genera taken from these rocks include *Laccopteris, Glenopteris*, and *Calamites*.

From Triassic sandstones in Rio Arriba County two fossilized species of *Equisetum* have been found. These are *E. abiquiense* and *E. Knowltonii*. The former has been more recently designated *Neocalamites virginiensis* and the second, although valid, would now be termed *Neocalamites Knowltonii*.

There exists no record of fossil Pteridophyta from the Jurassic in New Mexico.

With the coming of the Cretaceous Period, fernlike plants became more numerous in the state. Many of these are species which may be found living today either in New Mexico or elsewhere. Thus *Gleichenia rhombifolia* has been taken from the Mesa Verde formation, five miles northeast of Cabezon in Sandoval County; and a new species of *Dryopteris*, as yet undescribed, was found in the Fruitland formation of San Juan

---

[2] The data for this section on fossil Pteridophyta have been assembled by Dr. Stuart A. Northrop, Chairman of the Department of Geology, University of New Mexico.

County. *Aneimia hesperia, A. circutaria,* and *A. cuneata* were also found in the same formation in San Juan County.

Also found in San Juan County are *Asplenium neomexicanum, Onoclea neomexicana,* a probable species of *Selaginella,* and a *Pteridium*-like fern. From the Vermejo formation in Vermejo Canyon, Colfax County, comes an *Aneimia*-like fern; and from this same formation just north of the New Mexico-Colorado boundary a number of fossil ferns have been collected, including *Acrostichum, Aneimia, Asplenium, Gleichenia, Osmunda, Polystichum, Stenopteris,* and *Woodwardia.*

Although the Paleocene strata of northern New Mexico have yielded numerous dicotyledonous leaves, only a few ferns have been taken from these rocks, these including *Aneimia occidentalis* and *Dryopteris.* Similarly, the Pliocene in the Santa Fe formation two miles north of Contreras in Socorro County has thus far yielded only a species of *Equisetum.*

KEY TO THE FAMILIES OF PTERIDOPHYTA

1. Plants minute, free-floating; leaves not more than 2 mm. long.

4. Salviniaceae p. 105

1. Plants more than 1 inch long or wide, terrestrial or, if aquatic, rooting on the bottom.

 2. Leaves palmately 4-foliate (like a 4-leaf clover). 3. *Marsileaceae* p. 104

 2. Leaves various, but not palmately 4-foliate.

  3. Stems conspicuously jointed, hollow; leaves minute, scalelike, united into sheaths at the nodes; sporangia borne in compact terminal cones....................5. *Equisetaceae* p. 108

  3. Stems not jointed, solid; leaves various but not united into sheaths at the nodes.

   4. Leaves very numerous, 4-ranked or spirally arranged or branched, less than 1/4 inch long; stems creeping or erect, plants mosslike...............................7. *Selaginellaceae* p. 114

   4. Leaves fewer, more than 1/4 inch long; habit of growth various, never mosslike.

    5. Plants aquatic or amphibious, appearing stemless but the stem (corm) submerged; leaves simple, grasslike, hollow; sporangia borne within the expanded hollow bases of the leaves................................6. *Isoëtaceae* p. 112

    5. Plants terrestrial; leaves not grasslike, simple, lobed or compound; sporangia not borne within the leaf bases.

    6. Leaves divided into sterile and fertile parts, the latter strongly modified; sporangia borne in spikes or terminal panicles.........................2. *Ophioglossaceae* p. 99

    6. Leaves not divided into separate parts or, if so, both parts leaflike in appearance; sporangia borne on under side or margins of blades................1. *Polypodiaceae* p. 19

I. POLYPODIACEAE Fern Family

Sporophyte extremely diverse in habit, size, and structure; stems (rhizomes) creeping or erect, bearing scales or hairs; fronds circinate in vernation, divided into a stalk and a blade, the blade pinnatifid to variously pinnate, glabrous or with scales, hairs, or wax; fertile and sterile fronds, if separate, somewhat similar in appearance; reproduction by means of spores, these in stalked sporangia which are grouped in clusters called sori; sori on the under side of the leaf or marginal, round or elongate, often covered or surrounded by a thin scalelike structure (indusium), or more or less covered by the recurved margin of the pinnule (false indusium); gametophyte a green, flat, cordate prothallium.

This large family is distributed from the tropics to the arctic, being most abundant in tropical mountains. It contains about 170 genera comprising more than 7,000 species. The ferns are relatively unimportant economically, but many are highly prized as ornamentals.

KEY TO THE GENERA

1. Rhizomes (and blades) with hairs only; blades large, coarse, compound, subternate; sori linear, marginal.......................16. *Pteridium*

1. Rhizomes scaly.

    2. Fronds of two distinct kinds, the sterile ones shorter and with broader segments than the fertile ones...........14. *Cryptogramma*

    2. Fronds all alike or nearly so.

        3. Sori round or nearly so, appearing as distinct, small dots on the under side of the blade.

            4. Fronds pinnatifid to occasionally bipinnatifid...17. *Polypodium*

            4. Fronds once- or twice-pinnate to tripinnatifid.

5. Indusia absent; rhizomes slender, widely creeping.

3. *Gymnocarpium*

5. Indusia present; rhizomes various.

  6. Indusia peltate, i.e., attached at the middle.

    7. Sori in a single row on each side of the midrib.

5. *Polystichum*

    7. Sori in two or more rows................6. *Phanerophlebia*

  6. Indusia attached either laterally or beneath the sporangia.

    8. Indusia reniform, thick, conspicuous, attached at the sinus (notch)..................................4. *Dryopteris*

    8. Indusia not reniform, usually inconspicuous, attached beneath the sporangia or at one side of the sorus.

      9. Indusia attached beneath the sporangia and surrounding them, divided into fingerlike or filiform segments.

1. *Woodsia*

      9. Indusia attached laterally, hoodlike over the sporangia when young..........................2. *Cystopteris*

3. Sori elongated, oblong or linear to lunate, mostly confluent.

    10. Sori naked (i.e., indusium lacking).

      11. Sori submarginal to marginal; rhizomes multicipital except in 1 species which is short-creeping............................12. *Notholaena*

      11. Sori covering most of the under surface of the segments; rhizomes multicipital or widely creeping.

        12. Rhizomes widely creeping; blades conspicuously hairy.................10. *Bommeria*

        12. Rhizomes short, thick; blades waxy beneath.

9. *Pityrogramma*

    10. Sori covered by a true or false indusium.

        13. Sori not marginal, covered by a true indusium.

          14. Sori oblong to linear; fronds once-pinnate; stipes dark colored.

8. *Asplenium*

          14. Sori more or less curved; fronds bipinnatifid to twice-pinnate; stipes straw-colored.

7. *Athyrium*

13. Sori submarginal to marginal, more or less covered by the reflexed edge of the segments.

    15. Sori marginal and confluent, covered by the strongly reflexed, continuous margins of the segments; or sori submarginal and scarcely covered by the reflexed margins of the segments, which are white-waxy beneath..................................11. *Pellaea*

    15. Margins interrupted by lobing, mostly reflexed over the sori, sometimes modified and appearing as separate, large indusia.

        16. Blades membranaceous, glabrous, scaleless; pinnules fan-shaped.
        15. *Adiantum*

        16. Blades mostly leathery, hairy and/or scaly, except in *C. Wrightii*, which is glabrous to glabrate.
        13. *Cheilanthes*

1. WOODSIA

Rhizomes tufted, scaly, the scales linear-lanceolate with a dark central stripe; fronds clustered, membranaceous, erect or suberect, lanceolate to lance-ovate, widest at the middle, the blades once- to bipinnate-pinnatifid, rarely tripinnatifid, pubescent or subglabrous to somewhat glandular, nearly scaleless; stipes shorter than the blades, relatively stout, persistent; sori roundish, often confluent in age; indusium inferior, thin, cleft into broad or hairlike divisions at maturity, often hidden by the sporangia in age.

This genus resembles *Cystopteris*, but is easily distinguished by the inferior indusium breaking into lobes, in contrast to the inflated, laterally attached indusium of *Cystopteris*.

A genus of small ferns of moist, exposed, rocky situations, comprising 38 species inhabiting chiefly the northern and arctic regions. The name is a dedication to Joseph Woods, an early English botanist.

KEY TO THE SPECIES

1. Fronds bearing long, articulate, many-celled hairs on the midribs and veins beneath...1. *W. scopulina*

1. Fronds lacking articulate hairs, the hairs, if any, unicellular or glandular.

    2. Fronds somewhat pubescent to distinctly glandular; indusium breaking into broad concave lobes, lacerate at apex......2. *W. Plummerae*

    2. Fronds glabrate to sparsely glandular; indusium breaking into filamentous segments.

3. Segments of indusium numerous, much longer than the sporangia, flaccid, somewhat intertwined, often appearing beaded.

3. W. mexicana

3. Segments of indusium few, turgid, shorter than the sporangia, often concealed at maturity........................4. W. oregana

1. **Woodsia scopulina** D. C. Eaton, Canad. Nat. II 2: 90. 1865 Rocky Mountain Woodsia.

Rhizomes short, forming large tufts; fronds numerous, tufted, brittle, 2½ to 12 inches long; blades oblong-lanceolate to lanceolate, pinnate-pinnatifid or bipinnatifid; pinnae ovate or oblong to deltoid-lanceolate with 5 to 9 pairs of crenate-serrate pinnules, the surfaces of which (especially the lower) are glandular-puberulent, with few to numerous flat, long, septate hairs, these also on the rachises; stipes straw-colored to brown, their bases chaffy; sori round, the indusia deeply cleft into narrow segments with hairlike tips. The term *scopulina* means "on rock."

Found on rocks and in crevices. Distributed from Quebec to Ontario and Alaska and south to California, South Dakota, Utah, Colorado, Arizona, New Mexico, Oklahoma, West Virginia, Tennessee, and North Carolina.

New Mexico: Brazos Canyon, in northeastern Rio Arriba County; mountains north of Raton, Jemez Mountains; Black Range; Ice Caves near Grants.

2. **Woodsia Plummerae** Lemmon, Bot. Gaz. 7: 6. 1882. (Figure 2.)

Fronds lanceolate or broader, more or less pubescent, minutely but conspicuously glandular, 3 to 20 inches long, bipinnatifid to bipinnate, rarely tripinnatifid; pinnae triangular-oblong, the pinnules ovate, oblong, obtuse, crenately toothed; stipe bearing scales which diminish in size toward the apex; sori near the margin; indusium inferior, splitting into several broad, concave lobes which at maturity are lacerate at the apex.

This species is highly variable in its various habitats. In the West it becomes smaller, more glandular-pubescent. Growing on shaded ledges and rocky banks, often on loose granite, it

FIGURE 2. Woodsia Plummerae. (a) habit × ½, (b) pinnule showing young sori × 3, (c) pinnule showing mature sori × 3, (d) sorus × 10.

ranges from Texas to New Mexico, extreme southeastern Utah and Arizona, and southward into northern Mexico.

New Mexico: Magdalena and Burro mountains; hills west of Socorro.

SYNONYMY

Woodsia obtusa var. *glandulosa* D. C. Eaton and Faxon, Bull. Torr. Bot. Club 9: 50. 1882.
Woodsia pusilla Fourn. var. *glandulosa* (Eaton and Faxon) Taylor, Amer. Fern Journ. 37: 86. 1947.

3. **Woodsia mexicana** Fée, Foug. Mém. 7: 66. 1857. (Figure 3.)

Fronds broadly lanceolate, 2 to 12 inches long; pinnae triangular-lanceolate, the segments deeply lobed, the lobes with sharply dentate margins, the teeth ending in delicate semitransparent tips which are ciliate in young fronds, giving the margin a whitish-crustaceous appearance; indusium rupturing into many filamentous segments which greatly exceed the sporangia.

This species is usually found growing in the crevices of rocks, cliffs, and ledges, often on igneous rocks. It is strictly confined to the mountains of the Southwest, ranging from extreme southeastern Utah, Colorado, and western Texas to New Mexico, southern Arizona, and southward to San Luis Potosi and Vera Cruz.

New Mexico: Very widely distributed in the state reaching to the top of some of the mountain peaks: Organ, Dona Ana, Burro, White, Sacramento, Tunitcha, Zuni, Capitan, Mogollon, Magdalena, Sandia, Gallinas, Jemez, Santa Fe, Las Vegas, and Capulin mountains; Mt. Taylor; Black and Sangre de Cristo ranges; Sierra Grande; breaks of the Dry Cimarron River; cliffs in Paradise Valley and rocky walls of Corrumpa Creek, both north of Clayton; Cimarron Canyon; Ute Park; Brazos Canyon in northeastern Rio Arriba County.

Harrington and Durrell report that many of their central and northern Colorado specimens show varied intergradation with *W. oregana*.

SYNONYMY

Woodsia pusilla Fourn. var. *mexicana* (Fée) Taylor, Amer. Fern Journ. 37: 86. 1947.

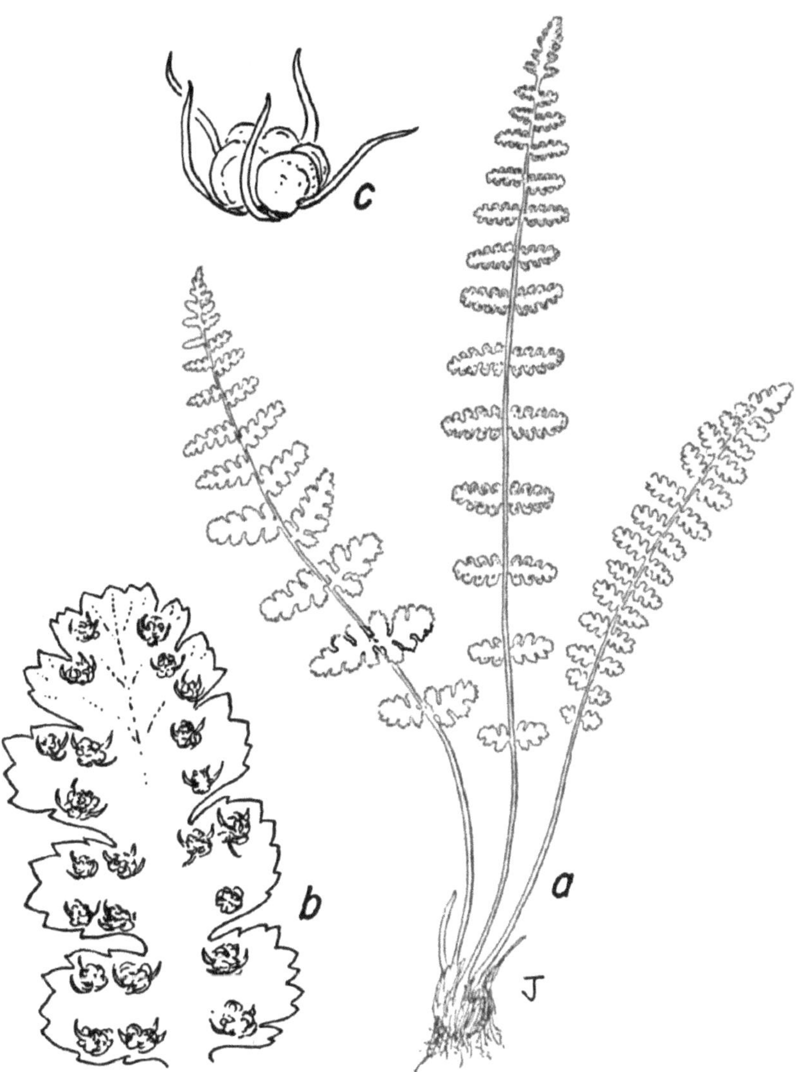

FIGURE 3. Woodsia mexicana. (a) habit × ¾, (b) pinna × 6, (c) sorus × 7½.

4. Woodsia oregana D. C. Eaton, Canad. Nat. II 2: 90. 1865. OREGON WOODSIA. (Figure 4.)

Rhizomes short; fronds tufted, 2 to 12 inches long, lance-oblong in outline; pinnae many, triangular-oblong, deeply pinnatifid into toothed lobes, the margins somewhat recurved, glabrate; stipes straw-colored above, darker below, smooth; sori submarginal; indusium rupturing into slender segments which are shorter than the sporangia and often concealed at maturity.

This species usually inhabits limestone cliffs and ledges, preferring a cooler and moister climate than do *W. Plummerae* and *W. mexicana.* It ranges from Quebec to British Columbia southward to New York, Michigan, southwestern Oklahoma, New Mexico, southern California, and northwestern Mexico.

New Mexico: Mt. Taylor, Lake Peak, and Apache Peak near Taos; Santa Barbara Canyon east of Penasco. It is believed that this species is to be found in some abundance in the northern part of the state.

2. CYSTOPTERIS

Rhizomes creeping, scaly; blades ascending or recurved, pinnate-pinnatifid to subtripinnate, ovate-lanceolate to linear-lanceolate, thin-membranaceous, glabrous, sparingly hairy on the rachis; stipes weak, slender, shorter than the blades, scaly at the base only; sori roundish, dorsal, separate; indusium membranaceous, hoodlike, attached on the inner side, at first covering the sporangium, early deciduous.

A genus of 18 species of different habit native chiefly to temperate regions. Small, delicate ferns of rocky, alluvial situations and woods, much resembling the genus *Woodsia* but easily distinguished by the type of indusium. The name is from the Greek, signifying "bladder fern," referring to the inflated indusium.

KEY TO THE SPECIES

1. Fronds narrow, triangular-lanceolate, the apex greatly elongated, basal pinnae the largest; rachis often bearing bulblets near apex.

1. C. bulbifera

1. Fronds broadly lanceolate, the apex short, acute, the basal pinnae shorter than the second pair; bulblets wanting............2. *C. fragilis*

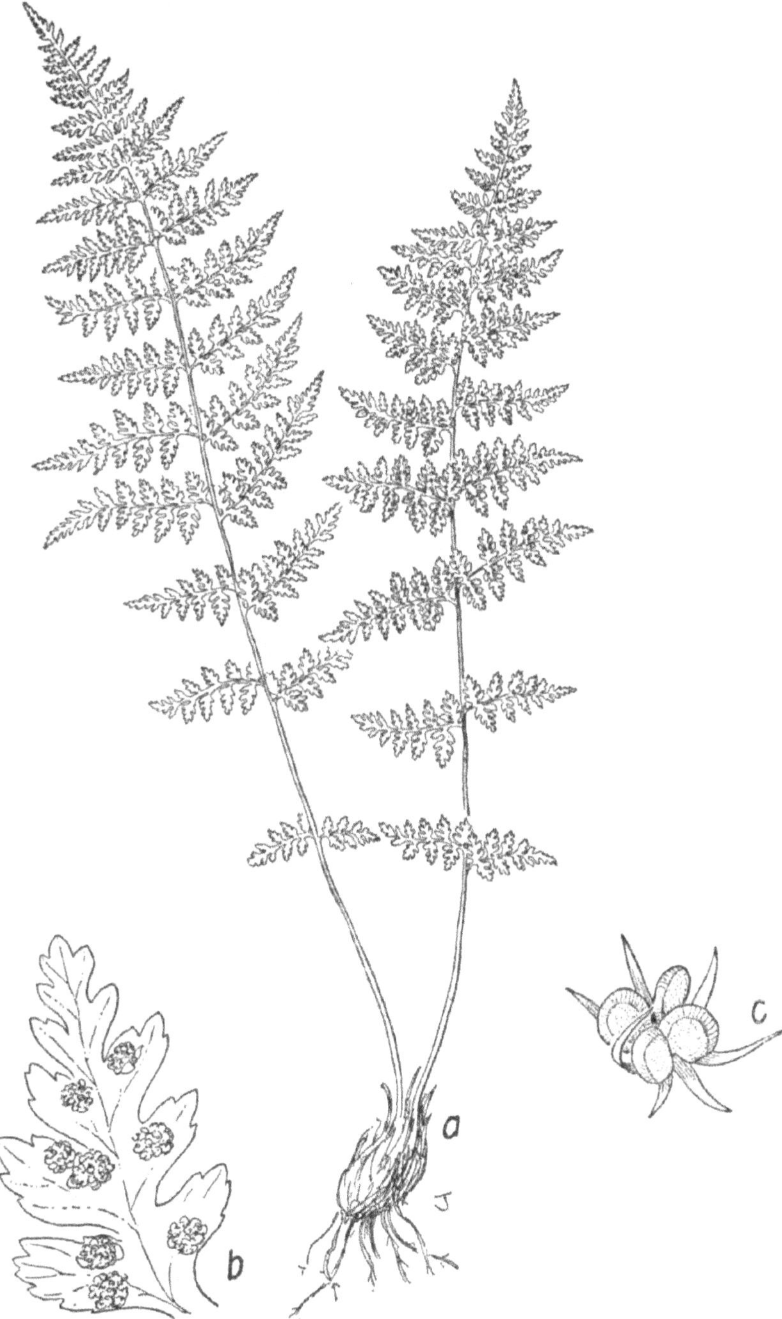

FIGURE 4. Woodsia oregana. (a) habit × ⅔, (b) pinnule × 6, (c) sorus × 6.

1. **Cystopteris bulbifera** (L.) Bernh., Schrad. Neues Journ. Bot. 1 ^{2}: 10. 1806. BULBLET BLADDER FERN. (Figure 5.)

Rhizomes short, somewhat scaly; fronds narrowly triangular-lanceolate, elongated at the apex, 12 to 36 inches long, nearly or quite twice-pinnate, the upper portion of the rachis and upper pinnae often bearing bulblets, these falling to the ground and vegetatively reproducing the plant; pinnae lanceolate-oblong, horizontal on the slender rachis, crowded, oblong, obtuse, toothed or pinnatifid; indusium truncate on the free side.

Shady slopes, rocky ravines, and moist, calcareous situations. Rather irregular in distribution from Newfoundland to Manitoba, New England south to Georgia and Alabama, west to Minnesota, and south to Missouri, Kansas, New Mexico, and Arizona; Utah.

New Mexico: Guadalupe Mountains, Twining Camp north of Taos.

SYNONYMY

Polypodium bulbiferum L., Sp. Pl. 1091. 1753.
Filix bulbifera (L.) Underw., Our Native Ferns, ed. 6, 119. 1900.

2. **Cystopteris fragilis** (L.) Bernh., Schrad. Neues Journ. Bot. 1 ^{2}: 27. 1806. BRITTLE FERN. (Figure 6.)

Rhizomes creeping; fronds several, variable, erect, spreading, glabrous, oblong to broadly lanceolate, 4 to 20 inches long, pinnate-pinnatifid to subtripinnate; pinnae and pinnules ovate-lanceolate, irregularly toothed or pinnatifid, mostly acute; stipes slender, shorter than the blade, brittle, with very deciduous scales near the base; rachis of pinnae winged, main rachis less so, greenish to straw-colored above, the stipe darker; sori small, rotund, not marginal; indusium convex, domed over the young sporangia, early deciduous, tapering and acute at the free end, the apex often toothed or laciniate.

The most widely distributed of all ferns, being nearly cosmopolitan, on moist soil of ledges, rocky slopes, and woods. Found from Greenland to Alaska, southward to New Mexico, Arizona, California, Texas, Oklahoma, Arkansas, and the Great Lakes region; Mexico to South America; Old World.

FIGURE 5. Cystopteris bulbifera. (a) habit × ½, (b) pinnule × 6.

FIGURE 6. Cystopteris fragilis. (a) habit × ½, (b) pinnule × 4½.

New Mexico: Widely distributed in the mountains of the state, reaching high altitudes. Organ, White, Mogollon, Sacramento, San Mateo, Lukachukai, Zuni, Sandia, Jemez, Santa Fe, and Las Vegas mountains; Black and Sangre de Cristo ranges; Mt. Taylor; Sierra Grande; Brazos Canyon in northeastern Rio Arriba County.

SYNONYMY

Polypodium fragile L., Sp. Pl. 1091. 1753.
Filix fragilis (L.) Underw., Our Native Ferns, ed. 6, 119. 1900.

3. GYMNOCARPIUM Oak Fern

A small genus of woodland ferns with long-creeping, slender, branched, scaly rhizomes, the scales few, glabrous, entire.

1. **Gymnocarpium Dryopteris** (L.) Newm., Phytol. 4 app. XXIV. 1851. (Figure 7.)

Fronds scattered, the blades membranaceous, triangular or deltoid; pinnae inclined upward, lower pinnae tripinnatifid, upper bipinnatifid to simple, scaleless, glabrous; basal pinnae articulate at base, nearly equaling the terminal portion of the blade; divisions of pinnae oblong, crenate to dentate; lowest pair of pinnae long-petiolulate, the pinnules on the upper side of the mature pinnae shorter than those on the lower side; stipe much longer than the blade, sparsely scaly toward the base, straw-colored; sori rather numerous, near the margin of the segments, rotund; indusium lacking.

A common fern of the northern and eastern woods which is generally found in deep, cool situations, it ranges from Newfoundland through Labrador to Alaska and southward to Virginia, Kansas, New Mexico, Arizona, and Oregon; Greenland; Eurasia.

New Mexico: Near Chama.

SYNONYMY

Polypodium Dryopteris L., Sp. Pl. 1093. 1753.
Phegopteris Dryopteris (L.), Fée, Gen. Fil. 243. 1852.
Dryopteris Linnaeana C. Chr., Ind. Fil. 275. 1905.

4. DRYOPTERIS Shield Fern

Evergreen, large, coarse, mostly woodland ferns with short-creeping, suberect and usually oblique, rather thick, densely

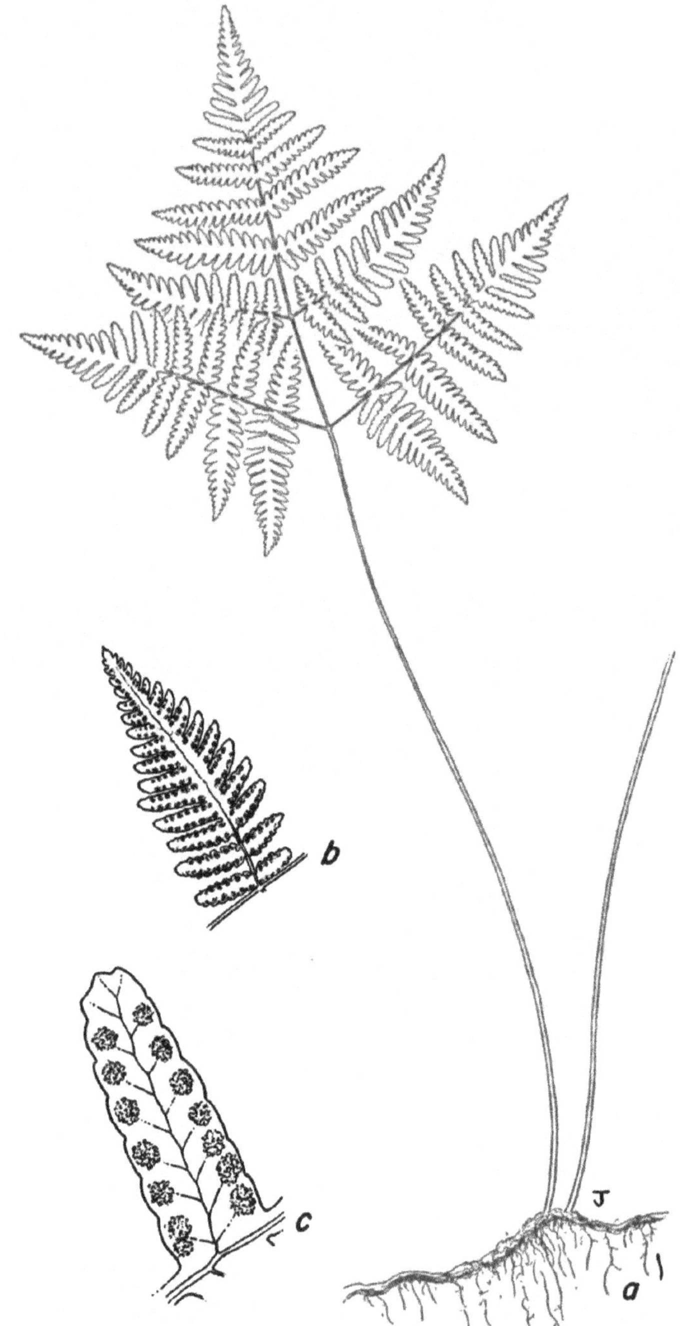

FIGURE 7. Gymnocarpium Dryopteris. (a) habit × ⅔, (b) pinnule × 1⅓, (c) segment of pinnule × 6.

scaly rhizomes, the scales broad and in many cases fimbriate; leaves tufted, lanceolate, and bipinnatifid (rarely simply pinnate), or deltoid and bi- to thrice-pinnate.

A genus of about 150 species mostly in the North Temperate region, many in eastern Asia and Africa, a few in tropical Asia and America. The name is from the Greek and means "oak fern."

1. **Dryopteris Filix-mas** (L.) Schott, Gen. Fil. 67. 1834. Shield Fern, Male Fern. (Figure 8.)

Fronds 12 to 32 inches tall, broadly oblong-lanceolate, nearly bipinnate, the blades narrowed at base, often reddish-brown-scaly beneath; pinnae short-stalked, lanceolate-acuminate; segments ovate-oblong, obtuse or acute, the ultimate segments toothed or incised, arising obliquely; midribs of the pinnae scaly, the midveins of the ultimate segments sparingly so; stipes straw-colored, stout, usually less than half the length of the blade, generously covered with large brown scales; sori round, in one row on each side of the midvein near the base of the segment; indusium large, conspicuous, thick, superior, round to kidney-shaped, attached at one side, not covering all the sporangia.

The herbalists derived from this species the drug aspidium, which has been widely used as a vermifuge, especially for tapeworm. It is a dangerous poison and dire consequences have resulted from overdoses. The species name is an old generic name meaning "male fern."

This fern has a wide distribution; it is found in rich, moist soils, in deep woods, on sheltered ledges, and in canyons. It occurs in Alaska and much of Canada, ranging from Newfoundland to British Columbia, south to Vermont, South Dakota, the mountains of extreme western Oklahoma, western Texas, New Mexico, Arizona, Nevada, Oregon, and the San Bernardino Mountains in California; Mexico; Greenland; Eurasia.

New Mexico: Organ, White, Sacramento, Elk, Jemez, Santa Fe, and Las Vegas mountains; Sierra Grande; Brazos Canyon in northeastern Rio Arriba County; Ute Park; base of massive, high, rocky ledge north of Beaverhead; bottom of deep crevices in lava beds south of Grants.

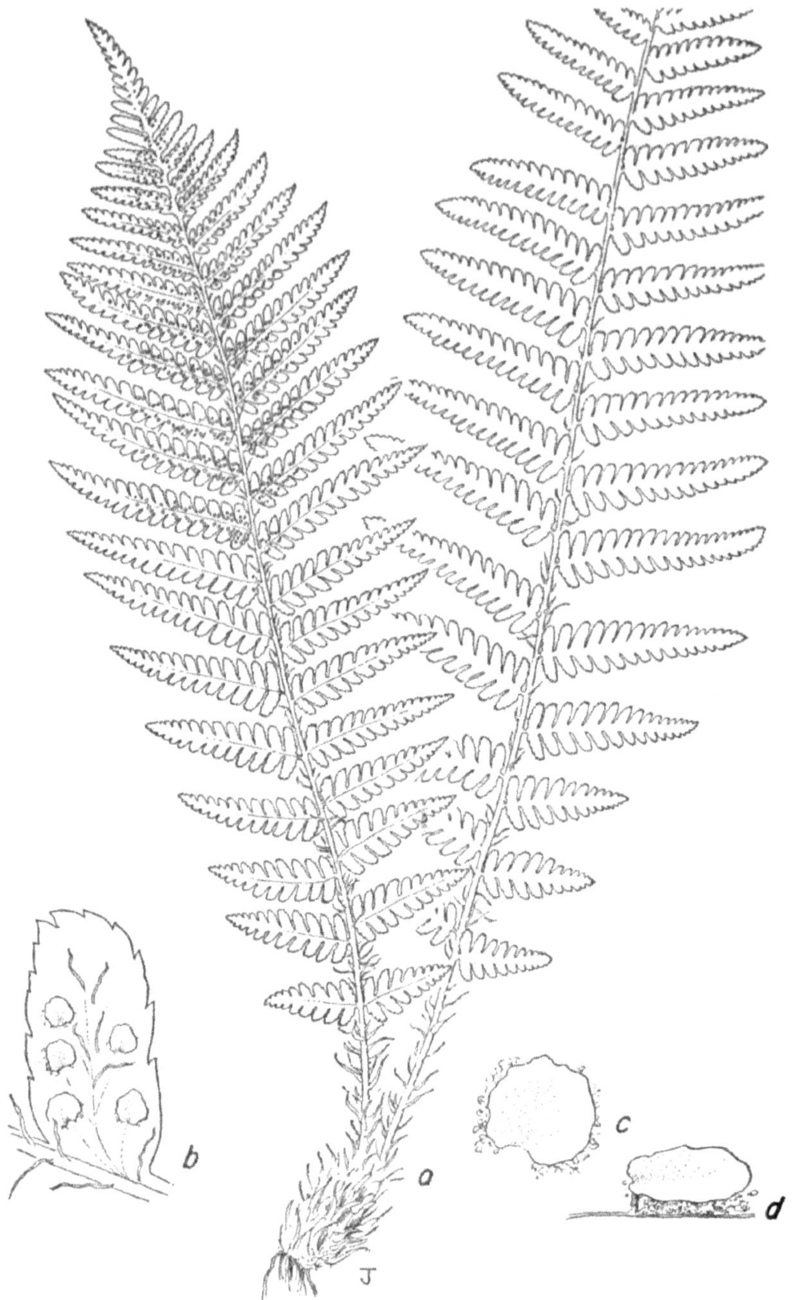

FIGURE 8. Dryopteris Filix-mas. (a) habit × ½, (b) pinnule × 3, (c) dorsal view of sorus × 7½, (d) side view of sorus showing lateral attachment of indusium × 7½.

SYNONYMY

Polypodium Filix-mas L., Sp. Pl. 1090. 1753.
Aspidium Filix-mas (L.) Swartz, Schrad. Journ. Bot. 1800²: 38. 1801.

5. **POLYSTICHUM** HOLLY FERN

Rhizomes usually thick, erect or suberect, densely scaly; fronds numerous, tufted at the end of a stout rhizome, 4 to 16 inches long, leathery, the blades once-pinnate; stipe much shorter than the blade, densely and persistently scaly, with a rather stiff, scaly rachis; sori large, round, and numerous, arranged in two rows, one row on each side of the midrib, often confluent in age; indusium entire or nearly so, orbicular, centrally attached, and persistent.

A genus of about 225 species widely distributed in the temperate regions. Some species are used as pot plants for indoor decorations, the most common being the Christmas Fern. The fronds of some of the species are gathered from the wilds and used in wreaths for funeral decorations. The name is from the Greek, meaning "many rows," referring to the sori.

1. **Polystichum Lonchitis** (L.) Roth ex Roem., Arch. Bot. 2: 106. 1799. MOUNTAIN HOLLY FERN. (Figure 9.)

Ascending rhizome stout, coarse, scaly, densely covered with old stipe bases and decaying fronds; fronds many, in clusters, rigidly coriaceous, once-pinnate, narrow in outline, tapering toward the apex and base; pinnae firm, sessile or short-stalked, somewhat sickle-shaped, acute, cut obliquely at the base of the lower margin, auriculate at the base of the upper margin, the margins serrate-dentate, the teeth spinulose-tipped; stipes short, stout, densely chaffy with lustrous, papery red-brown to chestnut-colored ovate to linear scales, as is also the whitish rachis although to a lesser degree; sori numerous on the upper pinnae only. *Lonchitis* is a name used by Pliny for a plant with a tongue-shaped leaf.

This species is closely related to the Christmas Fern, but is smaller and has more scaly stipes. It is found growing in deep shade of damp woods and often on shaded, calcareous cliffs and rock slides, in mountainous areas from Newfoundland to

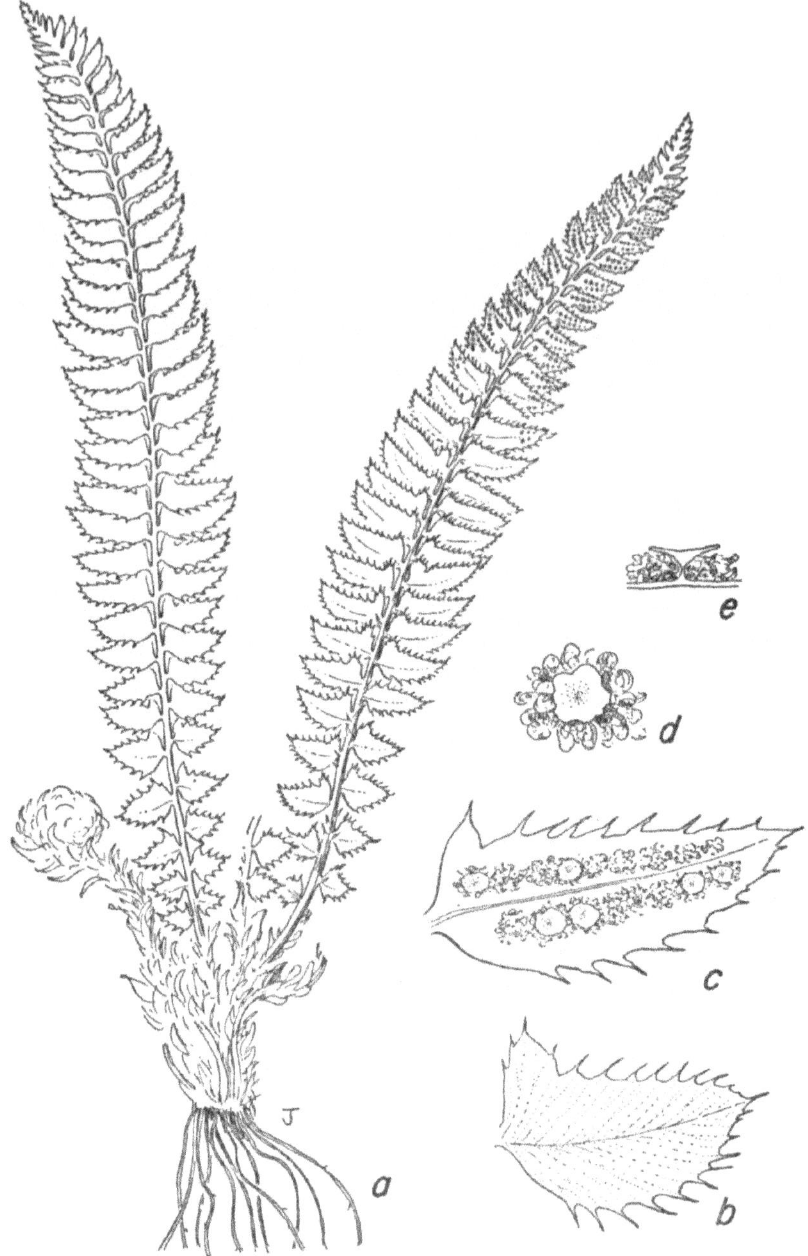

FIGURE 9. Polystichum Lonchitis. (a) habit × ½, (b) pinnule × 2½, (c) fertile pinnule × 3½, (d) dorsal view of sorus × 9, (e) lateral view of sorus showing centrally attached indusium × 9.

Alaska, southern Ontario, Michigan, and Montana, and in the mountains of Colorado, New Mexico, Arizona, and California; Greenland; Eurasia.

New Mexico: Although it has been reported from New Mexico by Harrington and Durrell[1] and by Flowers,[2] we have seen no specimens from the state.

SYNONYMY

Polypodium Lonchitis L., Sp. Pl. 1088. 1753.

6. PHANEROPHLEBIA

Rather coarse ferns of cliffs and rocky situations. Rhizomes short, thick, suberect, scaly; fronds clustered, rigidly ascending, simply-pinnate; leaflets 5 to 16, broad; sori round, mostly in 2 or more rows on each side of the midrib; indusia orbicular, peltate, centrally attached. A genus of about 20 species, it is found in Japan, Hawaii, South America, South Africa, Mexico, and southern United States.

The generic name is a combination of two Greek words meaning "visible veins."

1. **Phanerophlebia auriculata** Underw., Bull. Torr. Bot. Club 26: 212. 1899. (Figure 10.)

Fronds 4 to 18 inches long; pinnae alternate on the sparsely scaly rachis, often somewhat sickle-shaped, asymmetrical to auriculate at the base, sometimes irregularly dissected toward the base of the upper margin, serrate or incised, spinulose; stipe shorter than the blade, sparsely covered with light-brown scales; sori round, scattered in 1 to 2 rows on each side of the midvein on the back of the pinnae.

This species inhabits cool, damp crevices of north-facing cliffs and is found in isolated localities from western Texas to New Mexico, Arizona, and northern Mexico, nowhere abundant.

New Mexico: Organ Mountains.

---

1 *Colorado Ferns.* Fort Collins, 1950.
2 Bull. Univ. Utah v. 35, Biol. Ser. v. 4, no. 6, 1944.

FIGURE 10. Phanerophlebia auriculata. (a) habit × ½, (b) portion of pinna × 2½, (c) sorus × 15.

7. ATHYRIUM

Rhizomes stout, bulky, somewhat scaly; fronds erect, flaccid, clustered, spreading, thin-membranaceous; indusia present, often curved or hooked at apex.

Rather large, usually erect, graceful ferns. The genus contains about 180 species, mostly East Asiatic, a few in the American tropics and only one in New Mexico. The Greek name, meaning "shieldless," is of doubtful application.

1. **Athyrium Filix-femina** (L.) Roth ex Mertens, Roem. Arch. Bot. 2^1: 106. 1799. LADY FERN. (Figure 11.)

Rhizomes short, upright, rather massive; fronds 12 to 80 inches long; blade narrowed at the base and apex, bipinnatifid to twice-pinnate; pinnae numerous, lanceolate; pinnules often adnate to the secondary rachis, these oblong, serrate with incised lobes, the surfaces nearly glabrous, scaleless, and sparingly glandular; stipes straw-colored, thick, shorter than the blades, deeply grooved on 2 sides for most of their length; sori not marginal, oblong and somewhat boat-shaped, opening along the side nearest the midvein, often confluent in age.

A common and variable fern of moist woods. More than 300 forms and varieties have been described, but it is here listed as a composite species. It is widely distributed in North and South America and Eurasia. The plant found in New Mexico is var. *californicum* Butters, which ranges from Idaho and western Wyoming to Arizona and California.

New Mexico: The Lady Fern appears not to be widely distributed in the state, but when found in cool, shaded canyons or beside running streams or around springs it is very abundant. For example, on Willow Creek in the Mogollon Mountains it is very common at the stream's edge. White, Sacramento, Mogollon, Jemez, Santa Fe, and Las Vegas mountains; Sangre de Cristo and Black ranges; Brazos Canyon in northeastern Rio Arriba County.

SYNONYMY

Polypodium Filix-femina L., Sp. Pl. 1090. 1753.
Asplenium Filix-femina Bernh., Schrad. Neues Journ. Bot. 1: 26. 1806.
Athyrium Filix-femina var. *californicum* Butters, Rhodora 19: 201. 1917.

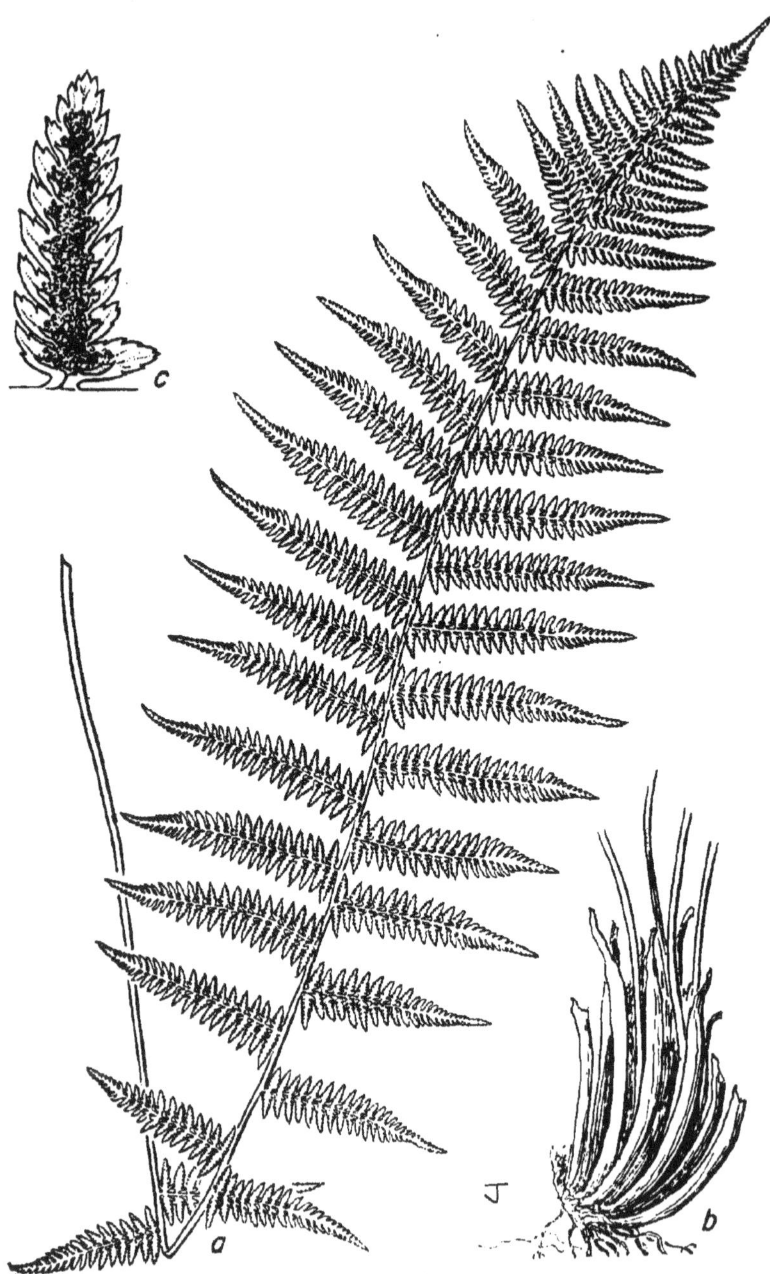

FIGURE 11. Athyrium Filix-femina. (a) frond × ½, (b) multicipital rhizome × ½, (c) lower surface of pinnule × 5½.

8. ASPLENIUM Spleenwort

Rhizomes suberect or sometimes creeping, scaly; fronds single or clustered, erect or spreading, various in size, lobed or once- to thrice-pinnate, thin or leathery; sori dorsal, oblong to linear, not marginal but borne on the veins oblique to the midrib; indusia attached laterally, thin-membranaceous, arching over the young sporangia and pushed aside at maturity exposing the sporangia.

A genus of some 650 species of terrestrial (often rock-loving) or epiphytic ferns widely distributed over the world. Five species occur in New Mexico; they vary from small, delicate plants to large, coarse ones. Many species hybridize in nature. (From *asplenon*, a name used by Dioscorides for an unspecified fern supposed to cure diseases of the spleen.)

KEY TO THE SPECIES

1. Pinnae few, linear to lanceolate; stipe greenish, longer than the blade; fronds densely tufted, grasslike....................1. *A. septentrionale*

1. Pinnae numerous, oblong to oval or broadly linear; stipe brown to black, much shorter than the blade.

  2. Pinnae oval to broadly oblong, often asymmetrical at base and somewhat expanded on the upper margin but not auriculate, usually not more than 6 mm. long.........................2. *A. Trichomanes*

  2. Pinnae mostly oblong, more or less auriculate at base on the upper margin, usually more than 6 mm. long.

    3. Fertile fronds usually recurved, sometimes rooting at the tips; pinnae opposite or nearly so.......................3. *A. Palmeri*

    3. Fertile fronds more or less erect, not rooting at the tips; pinnae opposite or alternate.

      4. Pinnae distinctly alternate on the rachis.....4. *A. platyneuron*

      4. Pinnae mostly opposite on the rachis............5. *A. resiliens*

1. Asplenium septentrionale (L.) Hoffm., Deut. Fl. 2: 12. 1795. (Figure 12.)

Fronds densely tufted, 2 to 8 inches long; stipes slender, much longer than the blades, naked, greenish except at the base; blades irregular, branching into 2 to 5 narrowly triangular to linear lobes; pinnae often curved, entire or toothed near the

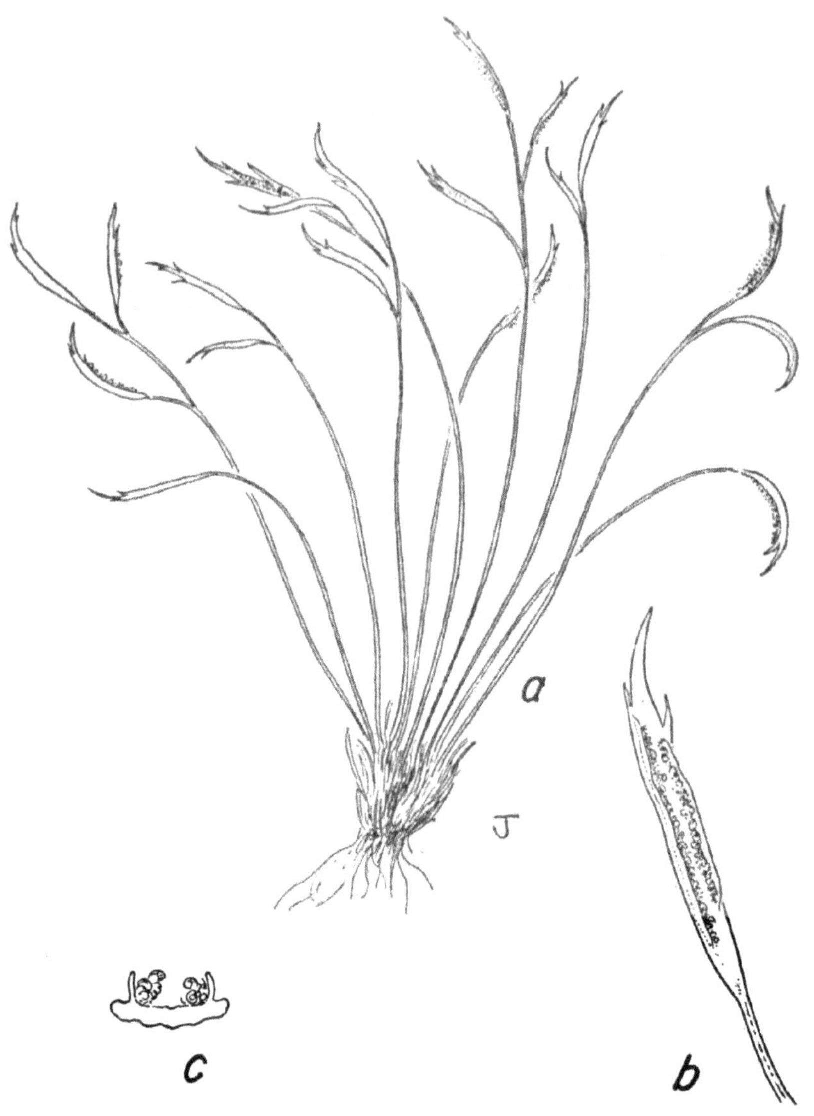

FIGURE 12. Asplenium septentrionale. (a) habit × ¾, (b) lower surface of pinna × 4, (c) cross-section of pinnule × 13.

apex; rachises without 2 sharp ridges on the upper side; sori usually in pairs, very elongate, 2 to 3 to the segment.

This fern, when dry, very much resembles a bunch of dry grass or sedge and is found in rock crevices and on ledges in mountain areas. Although it is distributed from the Dakotas southward in the Rocky Mountain states and from western Oklahoma to New Mexico, Arizona, Colorado, California, and northwestern Mexico, it is not a common fern. It is also found in the Old World.

New Mexico: Northern point of Llano Estacado; in lava of Cougar Mountain near Grants; Jemez and Las Vegas mountains; Sangre de Cristo and Black ranges, Sierra Grande; Ute Park; common in Brazos Canyon in Rio Arriba County in small crevices of large igneous boulders.

SYNONYMY

Acrostichum septentrionale L., Sp. Pl. 1068. 1753.

2. Asplenium Trichomanes L., Sp. Pl. 1080. 1753. (by pre-Linnaean botanists placed in the genus *Trichomanes*) MAIDENHAIR SPLEENWORT. (Figure 13.)

Rhizomes short; fronds many, 2 to 10 inches tall, in dense, radiating or one-sided spreading tufts, the plants with many denuded old rachises, herbaceous, simply pinnate; pinnae 15 to 30 pairs, the lower ones more widely spaced, mostly less than 6 mm. long, the breadth more than half the length, roundish-oblong, oblique, often broadly wedge-shaped at base and somewhat expanded on the upper margin but not auriculate, entire, crenate, or slightly incised, falling earlier than the stipes; stipe firm, threadlike, shiny purplish-brown; rachises with 2 sharp ridges on upper side; sori 5 to 6, elongate, when immature midway between the midrib and the margin of the pinnae, at maturity spreading over most of the dorsal surface.

Commonly found in shaded, calcareous crevices of cliffs and ledges, it is one of the most widely distributed of the spleenworts. It occurs from British Columbia and Nova Scotia to Alaska, southwest to Georgia, Tennessee, Alabama, Indiana, Oklahoma, Texas, New Mexico, Arizona, and Colorado; Old World.

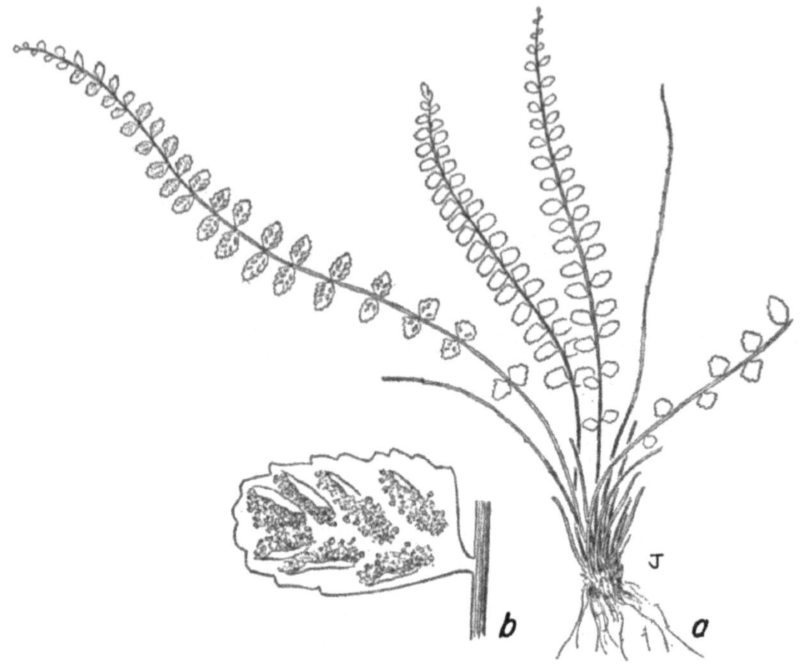

FIGURE 13. Asplenium Trichomanes. (a) habit × ½, (b) lower surface of pinna × 5.

New Mexico: Organ, Mogollon, Big Hatchet, Santa Rita, Jemez, Santa Fe, and Las Vegas mountains; Sangre de Cristo and Black ranges; lava beds east of Grants.

3. Asplenium Palmeri Maxon, Contrib. U. S. Nat. Herb. 13: 39. 1909.

Fronds 4 to 12 inches tall, narrowly lanceolate to lanceolate, the fertile ones usually recurved, some of them narrowed and rooting at the apex; pinnae opposite or nearly so, oblong, obtuse, toothed or serrate, nearly sessile; stipe and rachis smooth, shiny, dark purple to black; rachis with 2 sharp ridges on the upper side; sori elongate, often confluent in age.

This species grows on shady cliffs and in sandy woods from New Mexico and Arizona south to Mexico and northern Central America.

New Mexico: Our only listing for this species is from the Organ Mountains; however, it has been collected in Arizona, near our western boundary, and may well be found in other sections of New Mexico.

SYNONYMY

Asplenium parvulum var. *grandidentatum* Goodding, Muhlenbergia 8: 92. 1912.

4. Asplenium platyneuron (L.) Oakes ex Eaton, Ferns of No. Amer. 1: 24. 1878. EBONY SPLEENWORT. (Figure 14.)

Rhizomes short, scaly; fronds dimorphic, densely tufted, once-pinnate, the fertile fronds longer than the sterile ones, 8 to 20 inches tall; sterile fronds often inclined or lying on the ground; pinnae 20 to 50 pairs, distinctly alternate on the rachis, blunt, oblong, sessile, toothed or serrate on the margins, diminishing in size downward, the lowest becoming triangular, auriculate at base of the blade on the upper margin, rarely so on the lower one; sterile fronds with broader, shorter pinnae; stipes very short, lustrous, purplish-brown; rachises with 2 sharp ridges on the upper side; sori 6 to 12 on each side of the midrib of the pinnae, oblique and becoming crowded at maturity. *Platyneuron* means "broad-nerved," an inappropriate name.

A highly variable species, commonly found in poor and sandy soil among rocks and on ledges, it ranges from Ontario to Florida and westward to Oklahoma, western Texas, New Mexico, and Colorado.

New Mexico: Turkey Canyon, breaks of the Cimarron River in the northeastern part of the state.

SYNONYMY

Acrostichum platyneuron L., Sp. Pl. 1069. 1753.
Asplenium ebeneum Ait., Hort. Kew. 3: 462. 1789.

5. Asplenium resiliens Kunze, Linnaea 18: 331. 1844. ROCK SPLEENWORT, BLACK-STEM SPLEENWORT, or LITTLE EBONY SPLEENWORT. (Figure 15.)

Rhizome short with rigid, dull-blackish scales; fronds upright, broadly linear, once-pinnate, leathery; pinnae thickish and firm, oblong, entire, crenate or shallowly serrate, opposite

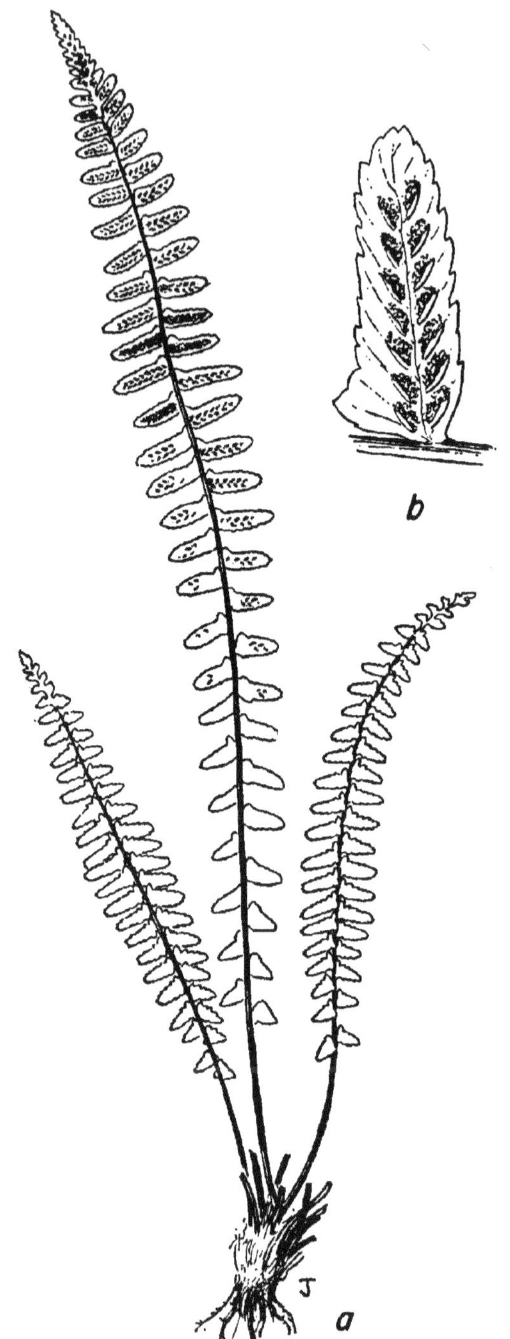

FIGURE 14. Asplenium platyneuron. (a) habit × ½, (b) lower surface of pinna × 3½.

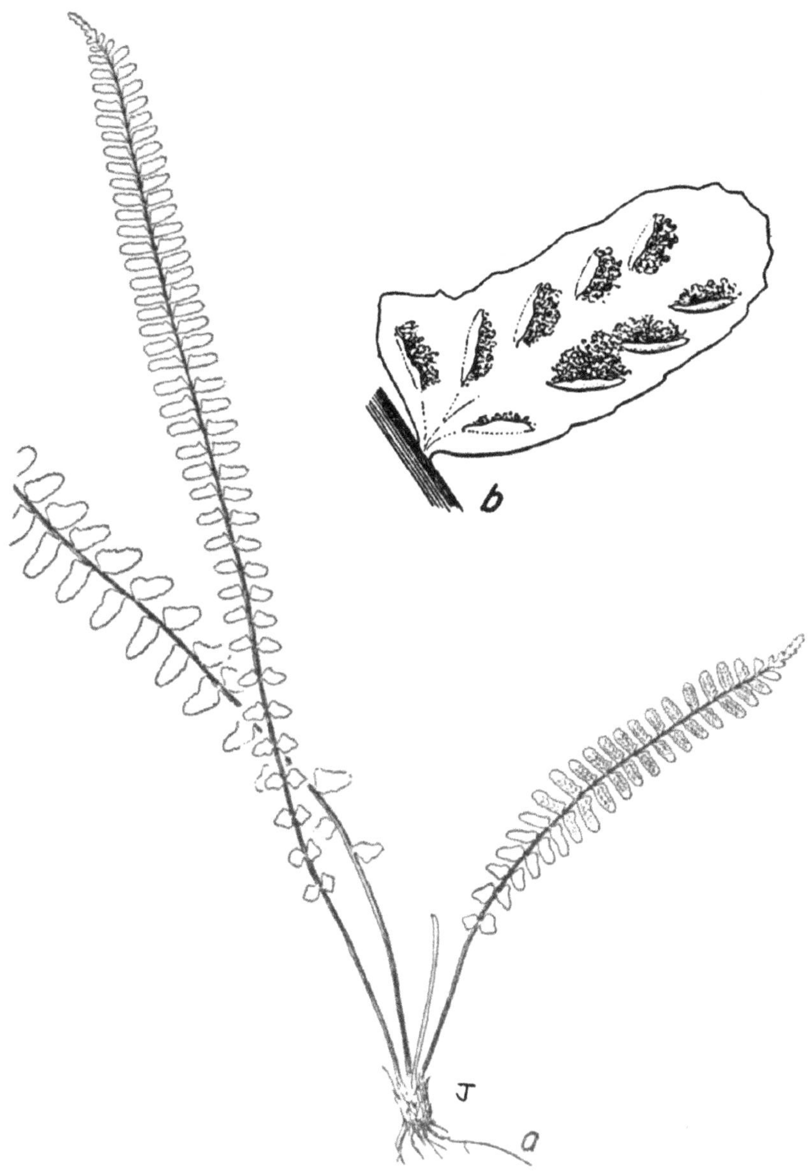

FIGURE 15. Asplenium resiliens. (a) habit × ⅔, (b) lower surface of pinna × 6.

on the rachis or nearly so and nearly sessile; stipe short, black or blackish; rachis with 2 sharp ridges on the upper side; sori short. The term *resiliens* means "recoiling."

Although closely resembling *A. Palmeri* and *A. platyneuron*, this species is distinguished from both by its short, stiffer pinnae which are slightly auriculate at the base.

Usually found growing among granite or limestone boulders and in shaded crevices of ledges and cliffs, it ranges from Pennsylvania southward to Florida and westward to Kansas, Oklahoma, New Mexico, Arizona, and along the Andean chain to Argentina.

New Mexico: Not widely distributed. Organ, Santa Rita, and Florida mountains.

SYNONYMY

Asplenium parvulum Mart. and Gal., Acad. Roy. Belg. Mém. 15^5: 60. 1842, not Hook. (1840).

9. PITYROGRAMMA Gold Fern

A genus of about 20 species, mostly American, some of which are extensively cultivated and often hybridize (the Silver Ferns and Gold Ferns).

Rhizomes suberect, short, thick, scaly; fronds clustered, uniform, tufted, once- to thrice-pinnate, covered by a white or yellow powder beneath, rarely hairy; sori often confluent.

The name *Pityrogramma* is from a combination of two Greek words and refers to the scurfy appearance of the sori.

1. **Pityrogramma triangularis** (Kaulf.) Maxon, Contrib. U. S. Nat. Herb. 17: 173. 1913. Gold Fern. (Figure 16.)

Blades thin, broadly triangular to deltoid-pentagonal, strongly tripinnatifid to subtripinnate, the lowest pair of pinnae large, nearly equaling the rest of the blade in size, the first or lowest divisions pointing downward and almost equaling in size the other pinnae on the main rachis; upper surface of blade green, glabrous to puberulent, lower surface white-ashy becoming brownish by the maturing sporangia; stipes at least twice as long as the expanded portion of the blade, scaleless, reddish-brown to purplish, shiny; sori small, numerous, confluent in

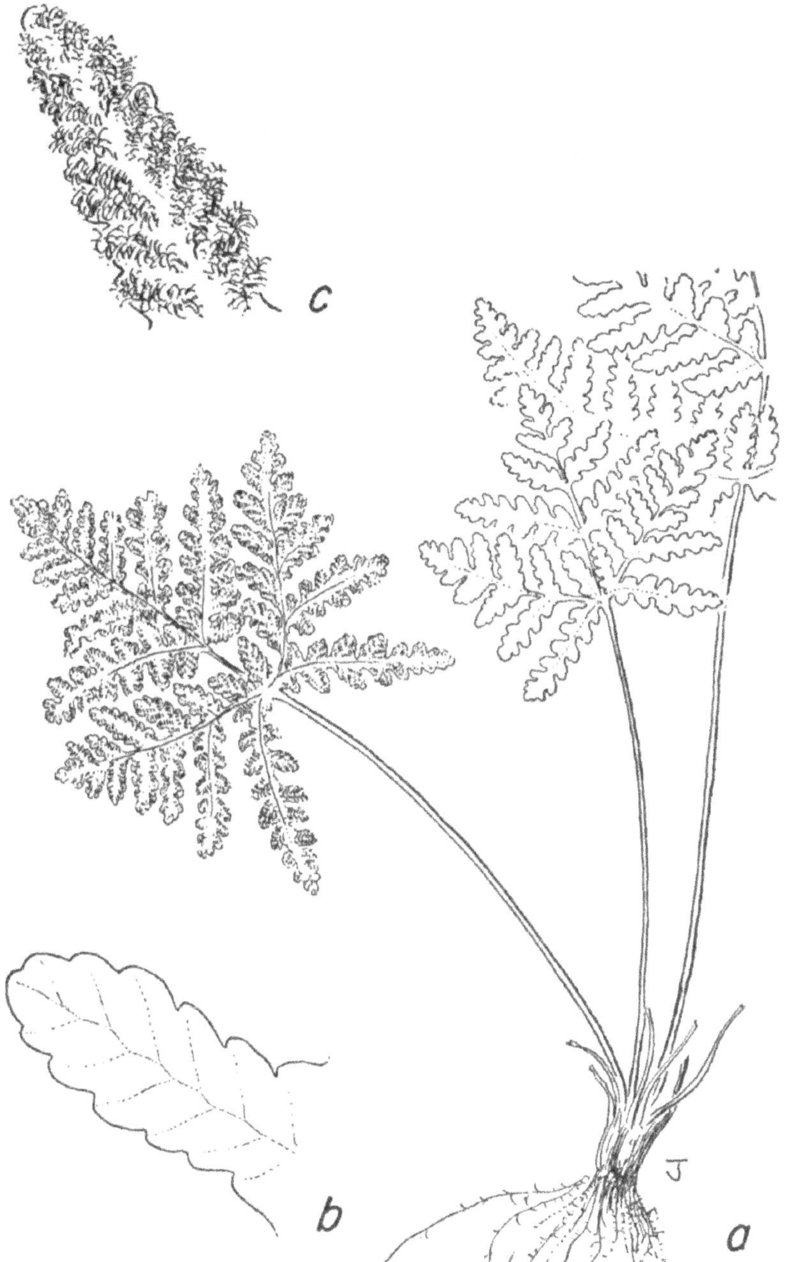

FIGURE 16. Pityrogramma triangularis. (a) habit × ¾, (b) upper surface of pinnule × 4½, (c) lower surface of pinnule × 4½.

age and almost covering the under side of the ultimate segments; indusium lacking.

This fern, which inhabits dry banks and ledges, ranges from British Columbia (Vancouver Island) to Nevada, southern California, Arizona, New Mexico, and northwestern Mexico.

New Mexico: Big Hatchet, Animas mountains.

SYNONYMY

Gymnogramma triangulare Kaulf., Enum. Fil. 73. 1824.

10. **BOMMERIA** Copper Fern

Rhizomes underground, cordlike, widely creeping, often branched, densely scaly.

A genus of 4 species found in the southwestern United States and Mexico.

1. **Bommeria hispida** (Mett.) Underw., Bull. Torr. Bot. Club 29: 633. 1902. (Figure 17.)

Rhizomes densely scaly, the scales linear-lanceolate, uniformly colored dark brown; fronds 4 to 10 inches long with the stipe accounting for nearly three-fourths of the entire length; blades pentagonal-deltoid, three- to five-palmately divided, tripinnatifid, the lower pinnae equaling the upper in size, the divisions pinnatifid to bipinnatifid, the upper surface of the blade olive-green, rather long-white-silky to hispid, the lower surface yellowish-green, long-silky to short-tomentose and sparingly scaly; stipes light reddish-brown, glabrous to sparingly pubescent, the main rachis winged throughout; sori small, numerous, confluent in age; indusium lacking.

Small ferns of shady, rocky ledges and dry situations. This species has a rather limited range from southern Arizona to New Mexico and western Texas; Mexico.

New Mexico: Organ, Florida, Guadalupe, and Bear mountains; Black Range; Mimbres River; 5 miles east of San Lorenzo, in northeastern Grant County.

SYNONYMY

Gymnogramma hispida Mett. ex Kuhn, Linnaea 36: 72. 1869.

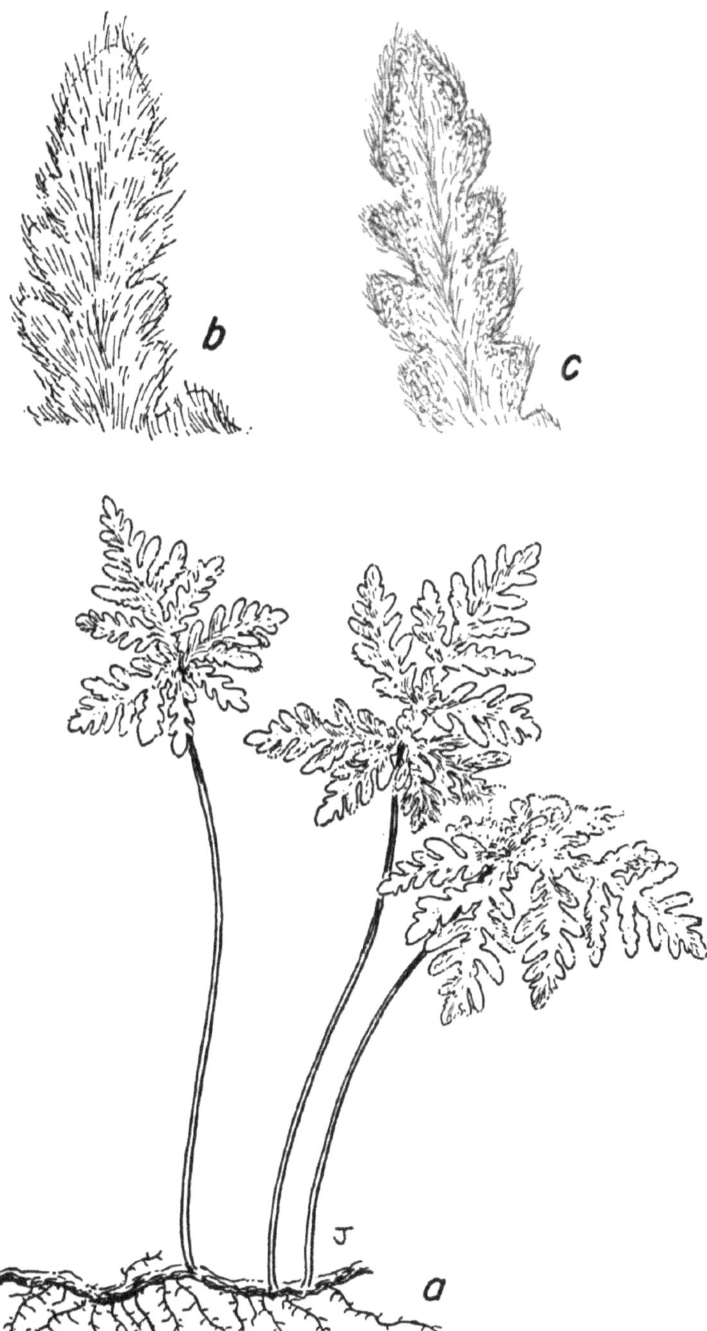

FIGURE 17. Bommeria hispida. (a) habit × ⅔, (b) upper surface of pinnule × 4, (c) lower surface of pinnule × 4.

11. **PELLAEA** CLIFFBRAKE

Rhizomes rather stout, multicipital, suberect (or long-creeping in *P. intermedia*), scaly; fronds erect, glabrous or occasionally pubescent on the rachises and midveins, once-pinnate to quadripinnate; segments scaleless, variable in shape and size, leathery; stipes wiry, pale brown to dark purplish; sori confluent, marginal or submarginal, in some species covered by a false indusium formed by the strongly revolute and sometimes modified margin of the segments, true indusium lacking in all species. *P. Fendleri* and *P. limitanea* are white-waxy on the under side of the segments.

A genus of about 80 species of rather small rock ferns. The name is from the Greek, meaning "dusty," which is a reference to the appearance of the stipe and leaves in some species.

KEY TO THE SPECIES

1. Rhizomes cordlike, widely creeping; stipes dusty-buff or pale brown
1. P. intermedia

1. Rhizomes thick, in clusters, suberect; stipes purple or black.

    2. Scales of the rhizome uniform in color, light brown to dark brown; pinnules without a distinct point at the tip.

        3. Blades pinnate above, often bipinnate below; pinnae and pinnules usually over ½ inch long.....................2. *P. atropurpurea*

        3. Blades 2- to 5-pinnate; pinnules 2 to 5 mm. long.

            4. Blades 2- to 3-pinnate, not waxy.............3. *P. microphylla*

            4. Blades 3- to 5-pinnate, white-waxy beneath; sori submarginal.
4. P. limitanea

            5. Blades 3- to 4-pinnate, the rachises branched but straight.

            5. Blades 4- to 5-pinnate, the rachises appearing zigzag owing to the peculiar forking of the branches..........5. *P. Fendleri*

    2. Scales of rhizome with a distinct black central rib; pinnules with a distinct short point at tip.

        6. Blades triangular-ovate; pinnae 4 to 10 pairs.
6. P. longimucronata

        6. Blades linear to lanceolate; pinnae 1 to 4 pairs or ternately divided......................................7. *P. Wrightiana*

1. Pellaea intermedia Mett. ex Kuhn, Linnaea 36: 84. 1869. (Figure 18.)

Rhizomes long, slender, creeping, branched, the scales with a dark, broad central stripe; fronds triangular to triangular-ovate, arising along the length of the rhizome, bipinnate; pinnules ovate, 3 to 10 mm. long; stipe and rachis stiff, wiry, dusty-buff to pale brownish; rachises short, hairy; sporangia at least partially covered by the false indusium formed by the recurved leaf margin.

This fern is an inhabitant of dry, rocky slopes and crevices of limestone cliffs and ledges. It is found from trans-Pecos Texas to southern New Mexico, southern Arizona, and into northern Mexico.

New Mexico: Black Range, Bear, Burro, Tortugas, Florida, Organ, Guadalupe, and top of San Andres mountains.

2. Pellaea atropurpurea (L.) Link, Fil. Sp. Hort. Berol. 59. 1841. PURPLE CLIFFBRAKE, PURPLE-STEMMED CLIFFBRAKE. (Figure 19.)

Rhizomes short, tufted, with long, rusty-brown scales of uniform color; fronds 4 to 15 inches long, usually once-pinnate above, twice-pinnate below, often remaining green throughout most of the winter; blades rather leathery, lanceolate or ovate-lanceolate to ovate; sterile segments entire to crenate, commonly oval or oblong, with a distinct hyaline margin; fertile segments narrow, mostly lanceolate, sometimes auricled, short-petioled, entire, glabrous above and below except for hairs along the midveins; segment margins rolled over the sporangia, the edges membranaceous and irregularly indented; stipes reddish-brown to dark purple, wiry, rather shiny; stipes, rachises, and rachillas more or less covered with slender, flaccid hairs, and somewhat scabrous.

A common fern of limestone and sometimes of sandstone ledges, it has a wide distribution from British Columbia, Washington, and South Dakota to Ontario and southward to Vermont, Florida, and westward to Oklahoma, Texas, New Mexico, Arizona, and Colorado; also in Mexico and western Guatemala.

New Mexico: Black Range, Bear, Organ, San Andres, San

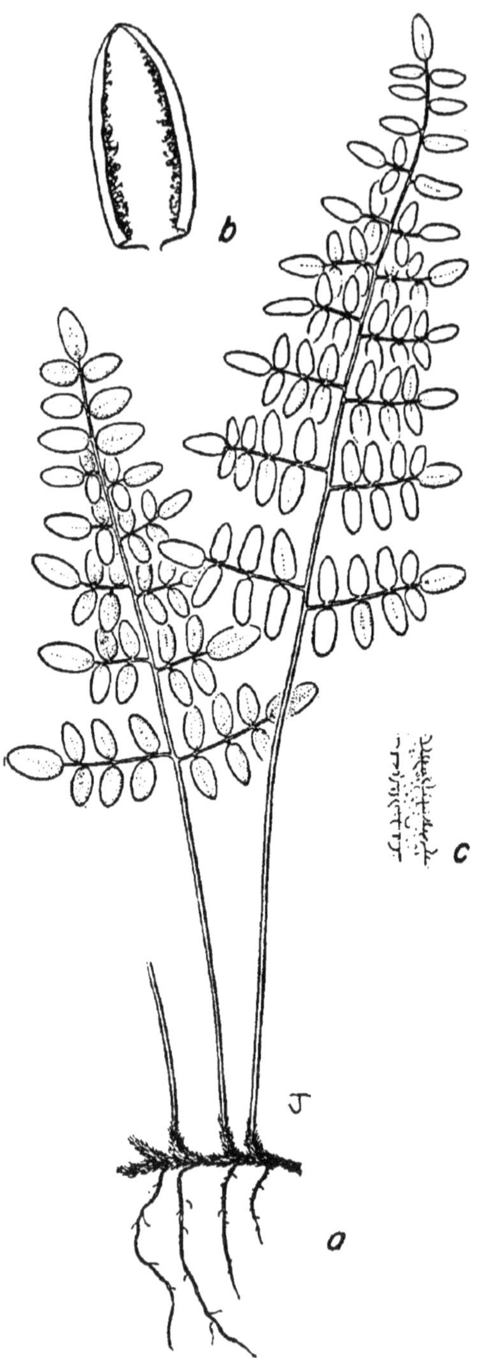

FIGURE 18. Pellaea intermedia. (a) habit × ⅔, (b) lower surface of pinnule × 3, (c) portion of stipe × 3½.

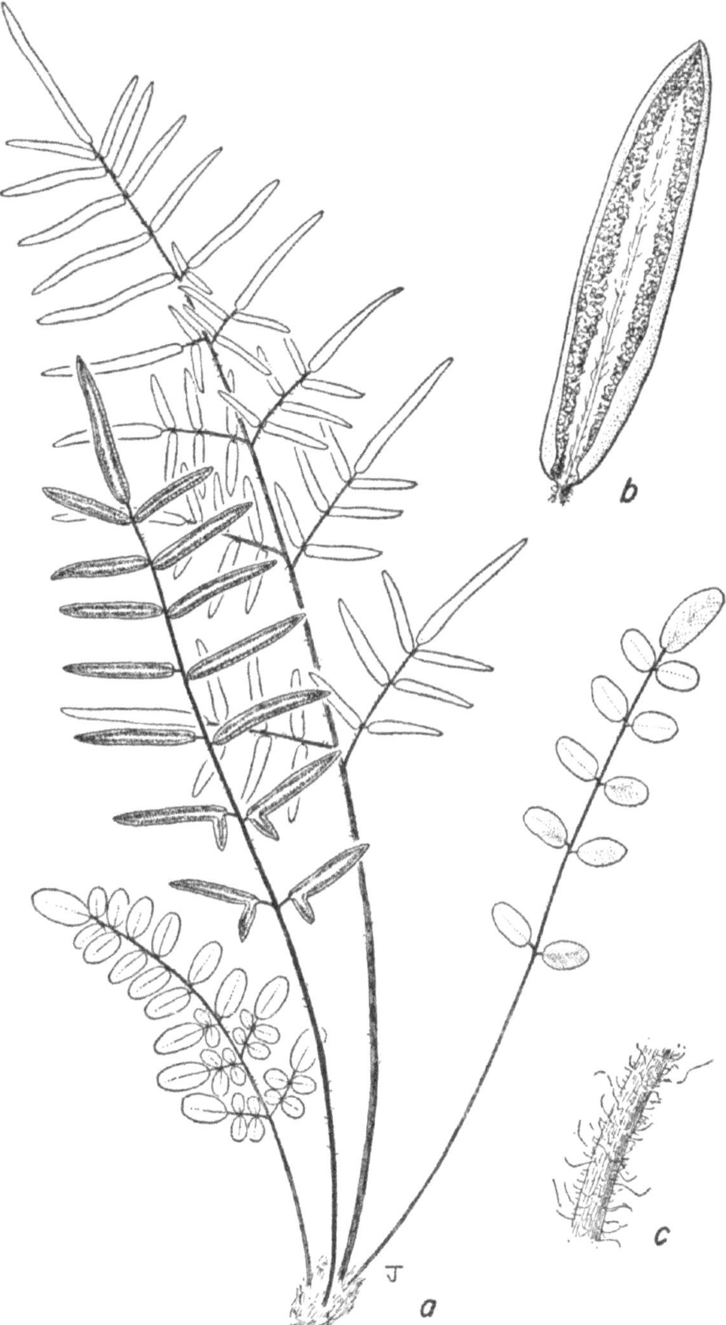

FIGURE 19. Pellaea atropurpurea. (a) plant showing sterile and fertile fronds × 1/2, (b) lower surface of fertile pinnule × 3½, (c) portion of stipe of fertile frond × 3½.

Luis, Guadalupe, Florida, and White mountains; Llano Estacado; cliffs of Corrumpa Creek in northeastern New Mexico; Mangas Springs.

P. atropurpurea (L.) Link. var. *simplex* (Butters) Morton (formerly known as *P. glabella* Mett. var. *simplex* Butters or *P. Suksdorfiana* Butters), occurs in parts of New Mexico. It differs from typical *P. atropurpurea* in its smaller size and glabrous rachises.

SYNONYMY

Pteris atropurpurea L., Sp. Pl. 1076. 1753.
Pellaea glabella var. *simplex* Butters, Amer. Fern Journ. 7: 84. 1917.
Pellaea Suksdorfiana Butters, Amer. Fern Journ. 11: 40. 1921.
Pellaea atropurpurea var. *simplex* Morton, Leafl. West. Bot. 6: 156. 1951.

3. **Pellaea microphylla** Mett. ex Kuhn, Linnaea 36: 86. 1869. (Figure 20.)

Rhizomes suberect, scaly; fronds numerous, clustered, bi- to thrice-pinnate, 4 to 8 inches long; pinnules very small, 1 to 5 mm. long, oval, ovate, or deltoid, often cordate at base; stipes wiry; rachises very slender; sori partly hidden by the infolded edges of the pinnules.

This fern, confined to limestone, is an inhabitant of cliffs and ledges, and ranges from northern Mexico northward to the southern escarpment of the Edwards Plateau in trans-Pecos Texas to southern New Mexico.

New Mexico: Guadalupe Mountains.

4. **Pellaea limitanea** (Maxon) Morton, Amer. Fern Journ. 40(4): 251. 1950. (Figure 21.)

Rhizomes short, stout, suberect, bearing brown scales; fronds ovate, triangular, up to 8 inches long, thrice- to quadripinnate; pinnules stalked, the ultimate segments minute, 1 to 4 mm. long, ovate to orbicular, pale green, glabrous to sparingly glandular-waxy above, densely white-waxy beneath; stipe and rachises dark purple to black, sparingly hairy to glabrous; sori small, submarginal, confluent, scarcely covered by the reflexed margin of the segments.

A small, delicate fern of dry limestone cliffs and ledges, it ranges from western Texas through New Mexico, southern Utah, Arizona, and southward to Mexico.

FIGURE 20. Pellaea microphylla. (a) habit × ¾, (b) upper surface of pinnule × 7½, (c) lower surface of pinnule × 7½, (d) cross-section of fertile pinnule × 7½.

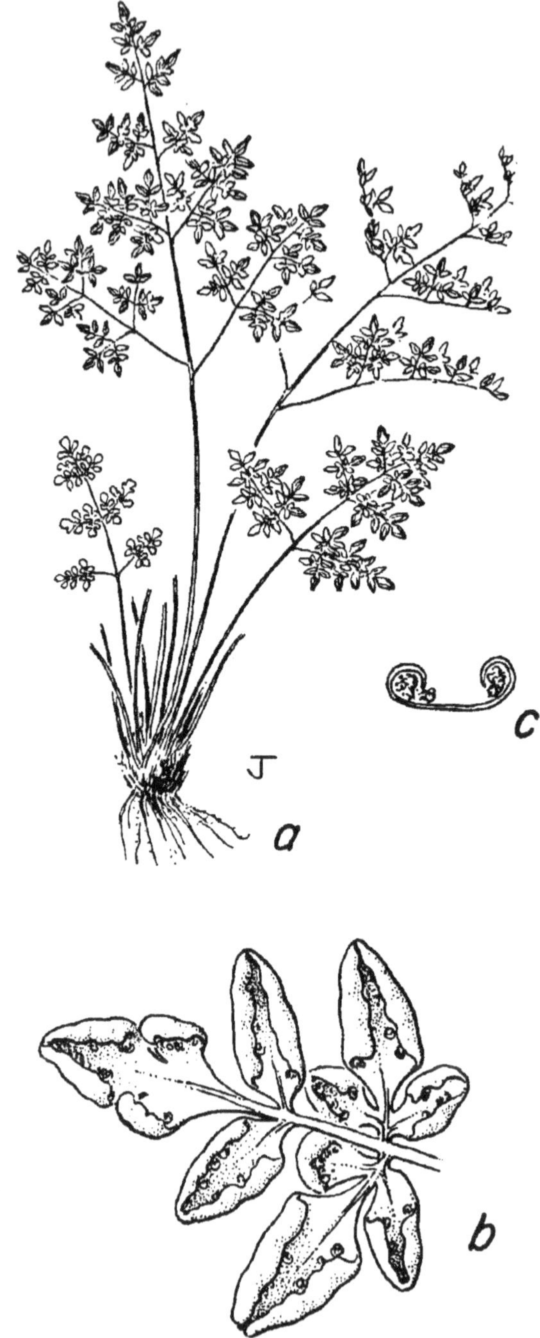

FIGURE 21. Pellaea limitanea. (a) habit × ¾, (b) lower surface of pinnule × 8, (c) cross-section of pinnule segment × 8.

New Mexico: Mogollon, Tortugas, Big Hatchet, Burro, and Organ mountains; Black Range. Also reported from Las Lagunitas near Las Vegas, San Domingo, and Sandia Mountains.

SYNONYMY

Notholaena limitanea Maxon, Amer. Fern Journ. 9: 70. 1919.

5. Pellaea Fendleri (Kunze) Prantl, Bot. Jahrb. Engler 3: 417. 1882. ZIGZAG CLIFFBRAKE.

Rhizomes stout, suberect, densely scaly; fronds densely tufted, 3 to 10 inches long, four- to five-pinnate; pinnae and pinnules alternate; ultimate segments narrowly ovate or elliptical, entire or asymmetrical at base, sometimes with 1 or 2 conspicuous.lobes at the base of the ultimate segments, white-waxy beneath, less so above; stipes dark brown to dark purplish-brown, somewhat wiry; rachises divaricate, zigzag; sporangia submarginal, elongate, partly covered by the recurved margins of the segments in youth but extending well beyond the leaf margins at maturity; indusium lacking.

Growing on dry cliffs and limestone ledges, this species ranges through Wyoming, Colorado, New Mexico, western Texas, and northern Mexico. It superficially resembles *Pellaea limitanea* but is more characteristic of colder and moister situations.

New Mexico: Sandia, Socorro, top of San Andres, and Jemez mountains; Black Range; Cimarron Canyon, near Santa Fe, and Santa Dona.

SYNONYMY

Notholaena Fendleri Kunze, Farnkr. 2: 87. 1851.

6. Pellaea longimucronata Hook., Sp. Fil. 2: 143. 1858. (Figure 22.)

Rhizomes short, tufted, suberect, the linear scales with a distinct blackish midrib and tawny margins; fronds 4 to 15 inches long; blades triangular-ovate or broadly lanceolate, bipinnate, the pinnae with 4 to 10 pairs of pinnules, sometimes a few ternately divided, all pinnules mucronate; sterile pinnules broadly ovate, and somewhat white-wavy-margined, the fertile ones smaller, narrowly ovate to linear lanceolate, the leaflets

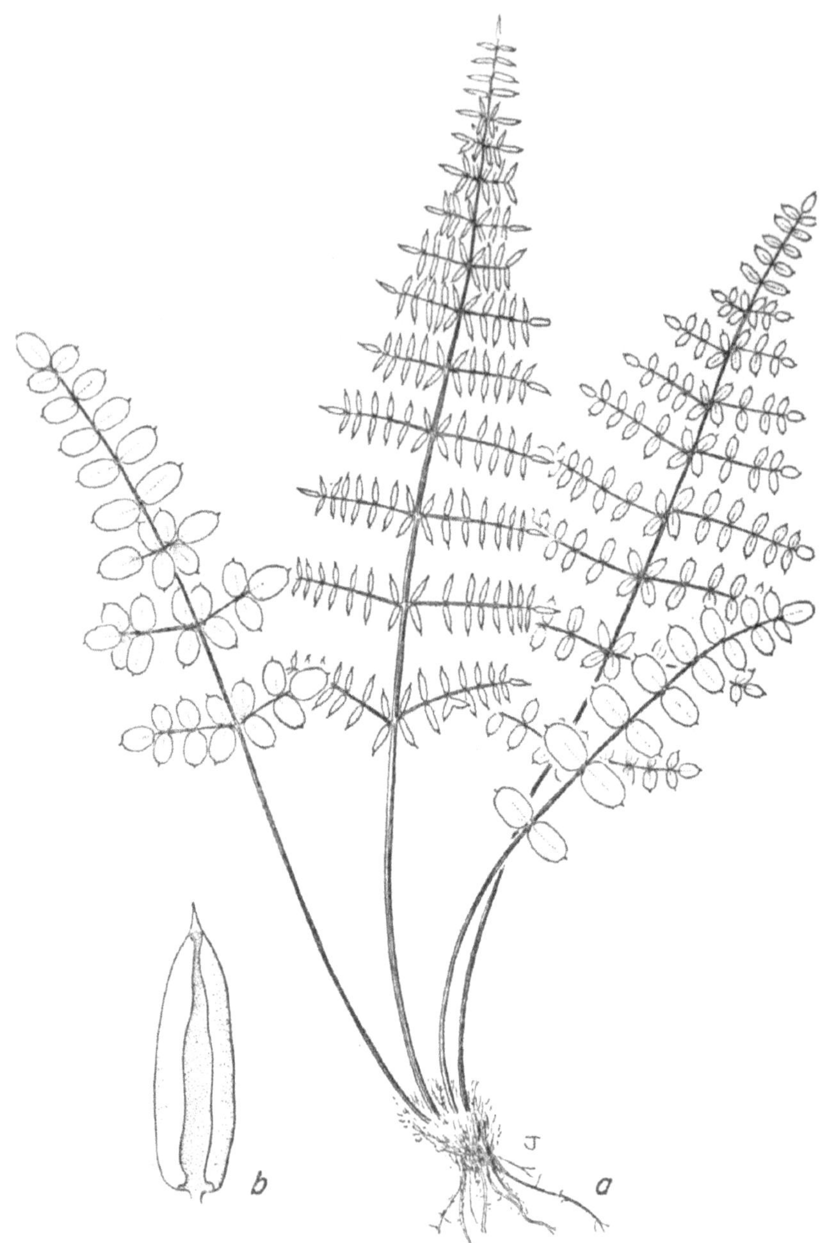

FIGURE 22. Pellaea longimucronata. (a) plant showing sterile and fertile fronds × ½, (b) lower surface of pinnule × 7½.

having a fine, powdery appearance; stipes and rachises dark brown or purplish-brown, wiry; sporangia hidden in part by the infolded margins of the pinnules, these extending back almost to the midvein.

This species and *P. Wrightiana* are sometimes found growing together; they are common on cliffs and rocky slopes. The range is from Colorado and Nevada to Arizona, New Mexico, and northwestern Mexico.

New Mexico: Black Range, Dona Ana, Organ, Burro, Guadalupe, Sandia, Florida, and Socorro mountains.

SYNONYMY

Pellaea Wrightiana var. *longimucronata* Davenp., Cat. Davenp. Herb. Suppl. 46. 1883.
Pellaea truncata Goodding, Muhlenbergia 8: 94. 1912.

7. **Pellaea Wrightiana** Hook., Sp. Fil. 2: 142. 1858. (Figure 23.)

Rhizomes erect, thick, densely scaly; blades 4 to 18 inches long; pinnae with 1 to 4 pairs of pinnules or ternately divided; sterile pinnules ovate, the fertile ones narrowly oblong to lanceolate, both mucronate; stipes short, dark brown to purplish-brown, wiry; sori partially concealed by the reflexed margins of the segments.

Chiefly in leaf mold and on igneous rocks, it ranges from southwestern Oklahoma and central Texas to New Mexico, Arizona, Baja California, and southward along the western Sierra Madre of Mexico.

New Mexico: Organ, Dona Ana, Burro, Florida, Socorro, and Sandia mountains; Black Range. It apparently has much the same range as *P. longimucronata* in New Mexico.

The New Mexican collections include specimens which previously have been identified as *P. ternifolia* (Cav.) Link, but which appear to be *P. Wrightiana.*

12. **NOTHOLAENA** Cloak Fern

Rhizomes short, congested, multicipital, suberect with abundant scales; fronds in clusters, rigid, once- to quadripinnate, thick membranaceous or leathery, linear to deltoid or pentagonal, tomentose, scaly, or white- or yellow-waxy or -powdery

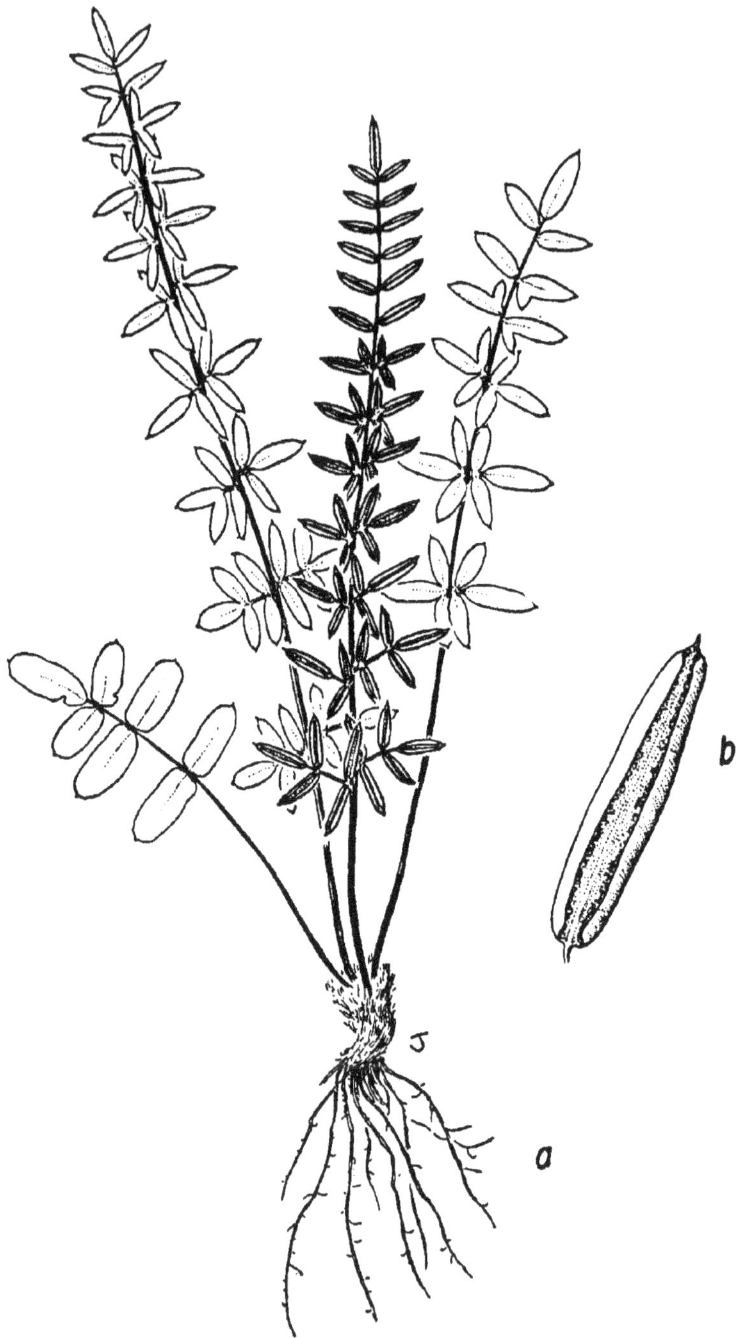

FIGURE 23. Pellaea Wrightiana. (a) plant showing sterile and fertile fronds × ½. (b) lower surface of fertile pinnule × 3½.

beneath; pinnae few to many pairs, the ultimate segments not beadlike; stipes (in New Mexican specimens) rarely longer than the blades (except in *N. Standleyii*), dark and wiry; sori mostly submarginal, roundish or oblong, sometimes laterally confluent; indusium wanting, the leaf margin not or only slightly recurved, not modified.

A genus of rock ferns, growing mainly in southwestern United States and Mexico, mostly xerophytic in habitat. It comprises about 60 species, one of which *(N. marantae)* is found in southern Europe. During dry, hot weather, the leaves frequently curl, and with the coming of rain they quickly expand and renew growth. One of the chief differences between this genus and *Cheilanthes* is that the former lacks the modified reflexed margin.

The name is from the Greek and means "spurious cloak," referring to the dense tomentum which forms a covering over the sporangia in some of the species.

KEY TO THE SPECIES

1. Blades pinnate or pinnate-pinnatifid.
    2. Pinnae regularly pinnatifid, villous above, densely tomentose beneath, not scaly...1. *N. aurea*
    2. Pinnae coarsely lobed or dentate, occasionally subentire, stellate-pubescent above, deciduous in age, densely imbricate-scaly beneath.
                                                        2. *N. sinuata*
1. Blades bipinnatifid to 2- to 4-pinnate.
        3. Blades pentagonal with 5 palmately divided, deeply pinnatifid pinnae...3. *N. Standleyii*
        3. Blades pinnately divided, with numerous ovate to lanceolate pinnae.
            4. Stipe brownish; pinnae glabrous or minutely dotted white-waxy above, white- or yellow-waxy beneath, scaly beneath, at least on midribs...4. *N. Grayii*
            4. Stipe blackish; pinnae hairy above, not waxy beneath, densely scaly and pubescent beneath............5. *N. Aschenborniana*

1. **Notholaena aurea** (Poir.) Desv., Soc. Linn. Paris Mém. 6: 219. 1827. (Figure 24.)

Rhizomes short, erect, covered with short dark-brown scales which have a light-tan margin; fronds several, of various lengths

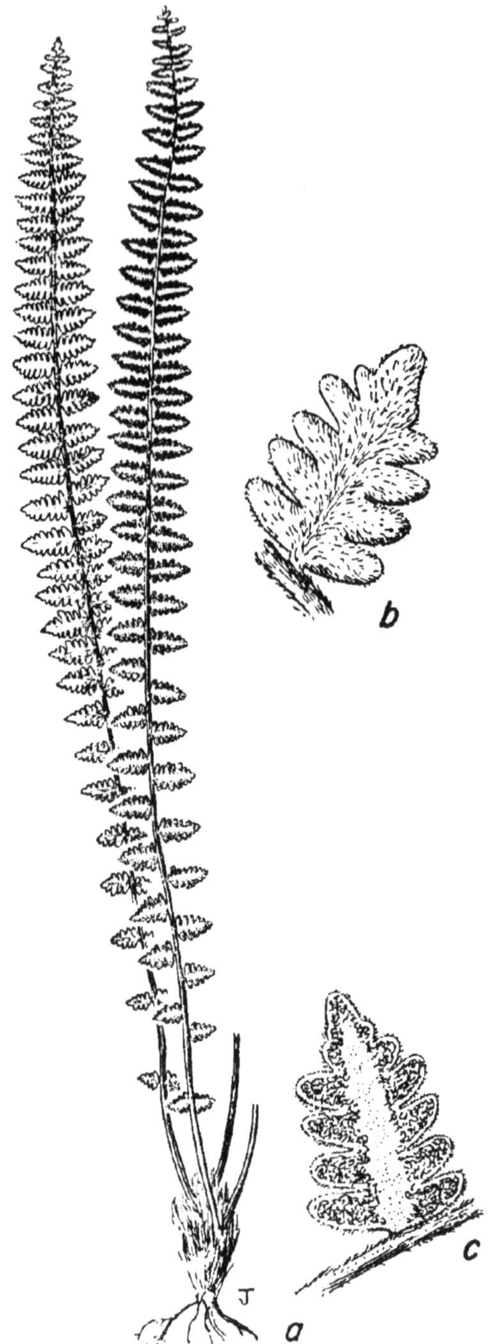

FIGURE 24. Notholaena aurea. (a) habit × ½, (b) upper surface of pinna × 4½, (c) lower surface of pinna × 4½.

in the same cluster, 2 to 16 inches long; pinnae crowded, ovate, 5 to 20 mm. long, slightly to deeply pinnatifid, dull green above, yellow-gray beneath; stipes short, covered with a dense yellowish pubescence which is deciduous in age; sori marginal, partly hidden by the dense tomentum.

An attractive fern of dry ledges and rocky slopes having a rather wide range from southern Texas, southern New Mexico, southern Arizona, and southward into Mexico and Central America to Ecuador and Argentina; Jamaica and Hispaniola. Palmer reported this fern as sold in the market at Saltillo, Mexico, a decoction of the plant being taken internally by natives for "pain in the stomach and coughs."

New Mexico: Organ and Dona Ana mountains.

SYNONYMY

Notholaena ferruginea Desv., Journ. de Bot. Appl. 1: 92. 1813.
Notholaena bonariensis (Willd.) C. Chr., Ind. Fil. 459. 1906.

2. **Notholaena sinuata** (Lag.) Kaulf., Enum. Fil. 135. 1824. (Figure 25.)

Rhizomes suberect, multicipital, covered with numerous, long, threadlike, light-brown scales; fronds suberect, once-pinnate, 4 to 15 inches long, folding together in dry weather (the whole frond then resembling a well-knotted stick), quickly unfolding after a rain; stipes short, scaly; sori more or less elongated, marginal, hidden by the light-brown scales.

Found in dry hills and rock crevices, often on limestone, it ranges from western Oklahoma, southcentral and western Texas to New Mexico, Arizona, southern California, and southward through Mexico into the Andean region to Ecuador, northern Argentina, and Chile; also occurs in Haiti.

New Mexico: Southern part of the state in the Black Range, Pyramid Peak, Three Sisters, Organ, Tortugas, Dona Ana, Florida, San Andres, Guadalupe, White, Big Hatchet, Bear, San Luis, Carrizalillo, Sacramento, Magdalena, Mogollon, and Tres Hermanas mountains; 30 miles east of Elk in southeastern Chaves County; Animas Valley; near Santa Rosa, and Lakewood in Eddy County. Reported from Las Lagunitas near Las Vegas by T. S. Brandegee.

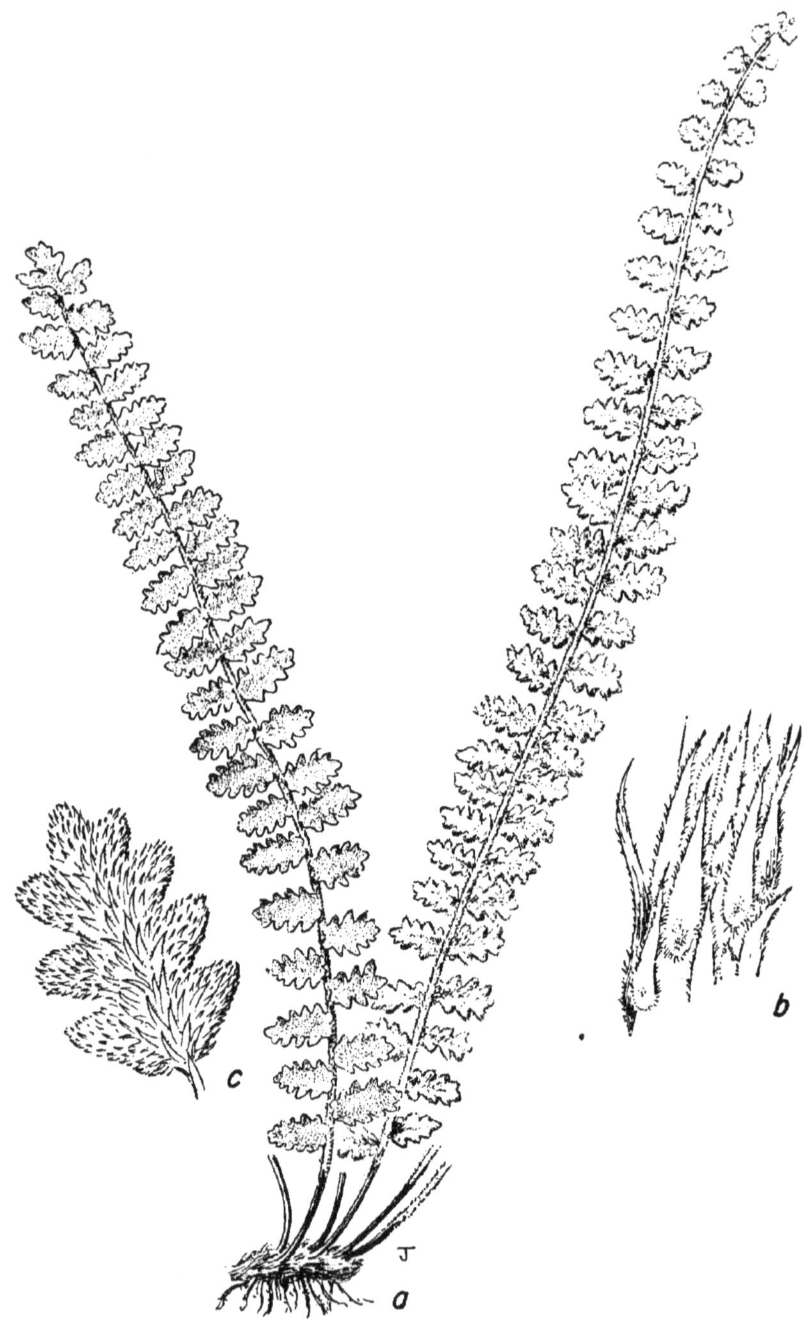

FIGURE 25. Notholaena sinuata (typical). (a) habit $\times$ 1/2, (b) scales on rachis $\times$ 10, (c) lower surface of pinna $\times$ 2½.

SYNONYMY

Acrostichum sinuatum Lag. ex Swartz, Syn. Fil. 14. 1806.

KEY TO THE VARIETIES (after Weatherby)[1]

1. Pinnae 1 cm. long or more, ovate, commonly subacute and with 4 to 6 pairs of oblong lobes; scales of upper surface of the blade with a narrow central portion or reduced to stellate processes, usually soon deciduous. Rhizome scales pectinate-ciliate or serrulate........*N. sinuata* (typical)

1. Pinnae mostly less than 1 cm. long, very obtuse, entire or with 1 to 3 pairs of broadly ovate lobes; scales of upper surface with a relatively broad central portion, usually persistent until full maturity of the frond. (2).

    2. Pinnae oblong, entire or with about 3 pairs of shallow lobes; rhizome scales pectinate-ciliate or serrulate..................var. *integerrima*

    2. Pinnae subquadrate, nearly or quite as wide as long, with 1 or 2 (3) pairs of lobes; rhizome scales entire or nearly so......var. *cochisensis*

Var. *cochisensis* (Goodding) Weatherby (Figure 26) has much the same distribution in New Mexico as does *N. sinuata* (typical). However, var. *integerrima* Hook. seems to be of quite limited occurrence, our only collection being from the Guadalupe Mountains. There is experimental evidence that *cochisensis* is toxic to sheep and goats while the typical variety is not.

3. Notholaena Standleyii Maxon, Amer. Fern Journ. 5: 1. 1915. STAR CLOAK FERN. (Figure 27.)

Rhizomes short, knoblike, covered with short, rigid darkbrown scales; fronds clustered, 4 to 10 inches long; blades pentagonal or star-shaped, bipinnatifid to tripinnatifid, each blade with 3 main divisions, the lower pair longer, each bearing an elongated pinnatifid segment near its base, blue-green above, white- or yellow-powdery beneath, curling into a knot when dry and expanding after rain; stipes much longer than the blades, brownish, wiry, brittle; sori marginal, but little covered by the reflexed unmodified margin of the segments.

A distinctive, attractive fern of dry, rocky slopes and canyons, it ranges from Texas and western Oklahoma, New Mexico, Arizona, southeastern Colorado, and Nevada, southward through western Mexico.

---

1 Johnston, Ivan M., Journ. Arnold Arbor. 24: 306-339, 375-421. 1943. (Pteridophyta by C. A. Weatherby).

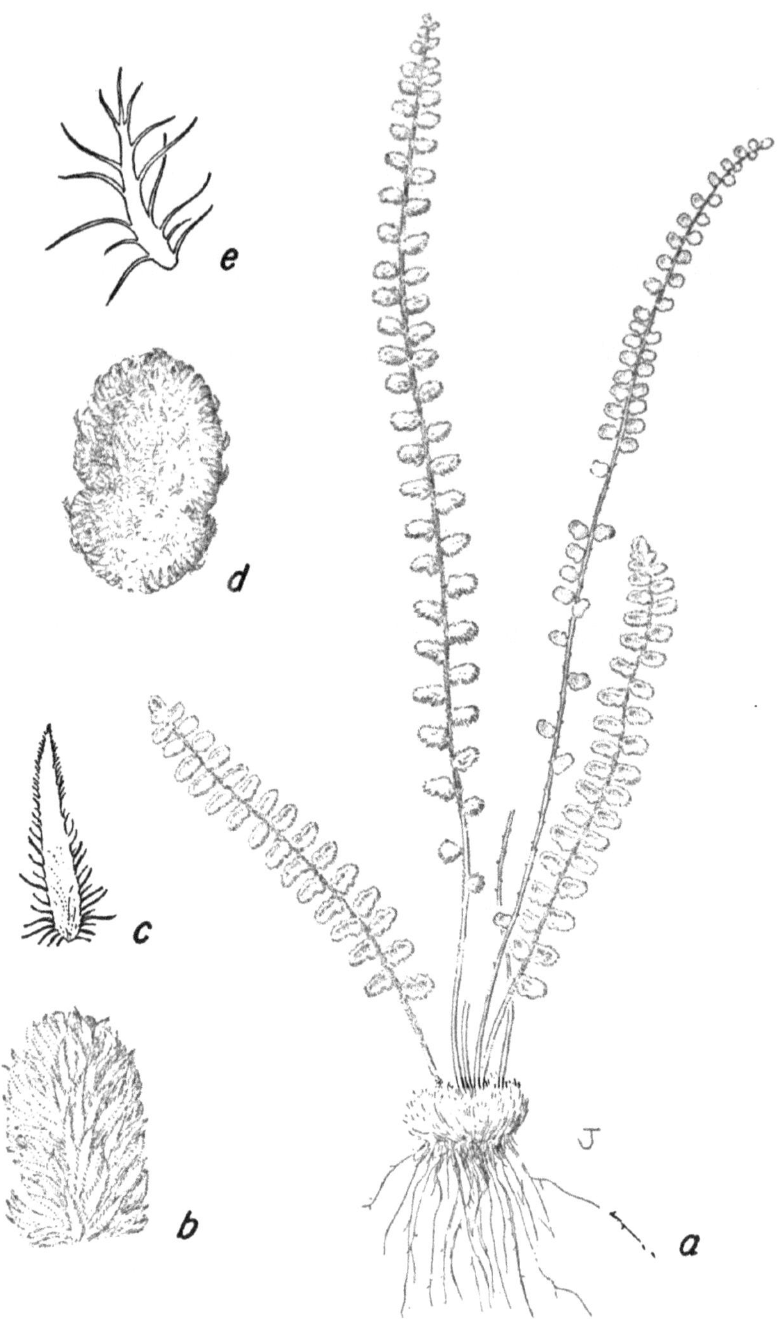

FIGURE 26. Notholaena sinuata var. cochisensis. (a) habit × ⅔, (b) lower surface of pinna × 6, (c) scale from lower surface of pinna × 19, (d) upper surface of pinna × 6, (e) scale from upper surface of pinna × 30.

FIGURE 27. Notholaena Standleyii. (a) habit × ⅔. (b) lower surface of pinnule × 7, (c) cross-section of pinnule × 7.

New Mexico: It occurs throughout most of the state although our records are chiefly from specimens taken in the southern half of the state including Socorro, Burro, San Luis, Tres Hermanas, Florida, Organ, Dona Ana, and Big Hatchet mountains; Black Range; also lava beds west of Carrizozo. In the northern part of the state specimens have been taken near Santa Fe and Las Vegas and in the Jemez Mountains.

SYNONYMY

Notholaena Hookeri D. C. Eaton, U. S. Surv. 100th Merid. Rpt. 6: 308. 1879, not Lowe, 1856.

4. Notholaena Grayii Davenp., Bull. Torr. Bot. Club 7: 50. 1880. (Figure 28.)

Rhizomes short-creeping; fronds many, clustered in a short row, 2 to 8 inches long; pinnae ½ to 1 inch long, triangular to triangular-lanceolate, pinnatifid to pinnate, not hairy but light green above, dotted-mealy and white-waxy beneath, bearing brown scales on the midveins; stipes brownish, ¼ to ½ the length of the entire frond; rachis light brown, bearing numerous elongated yellow-brown scales; sori marginal, partly hidden by the reflexed margins of the segments.

A small fern of dry, rocky slopes and ledges. Rather local in distribution, it ranges through western Texas, Arizona, and northern Mexico. We have no record of any specimens collected in the state, but it has been collected across the border in Arizona and is within the New Mexican range.

SYNONYMY

Notholaena hypoleuca Goodding, Muhlenbergia 8: 24. 1912.

5. Notholaena Aschenborniana Klotzsch, Linnaea 20: 417. 1847. (Figure 29.)

Rhizomes short; fronds narrowly ovate-lanceolate, 8 to 12 inches long, bipinnate; pinnae 1 to 1½ inches long, lanceolate to linear-oblong, thinly stellate-pubescent above, densely imbricate-scaly and hairy beneath, olive-green above, brown beneath; stipe blackish, stout, pectinate-scaly.

Found on dry, rocky slopes and ledges, it ranges from western Texas and Arizona, south into Mexico.

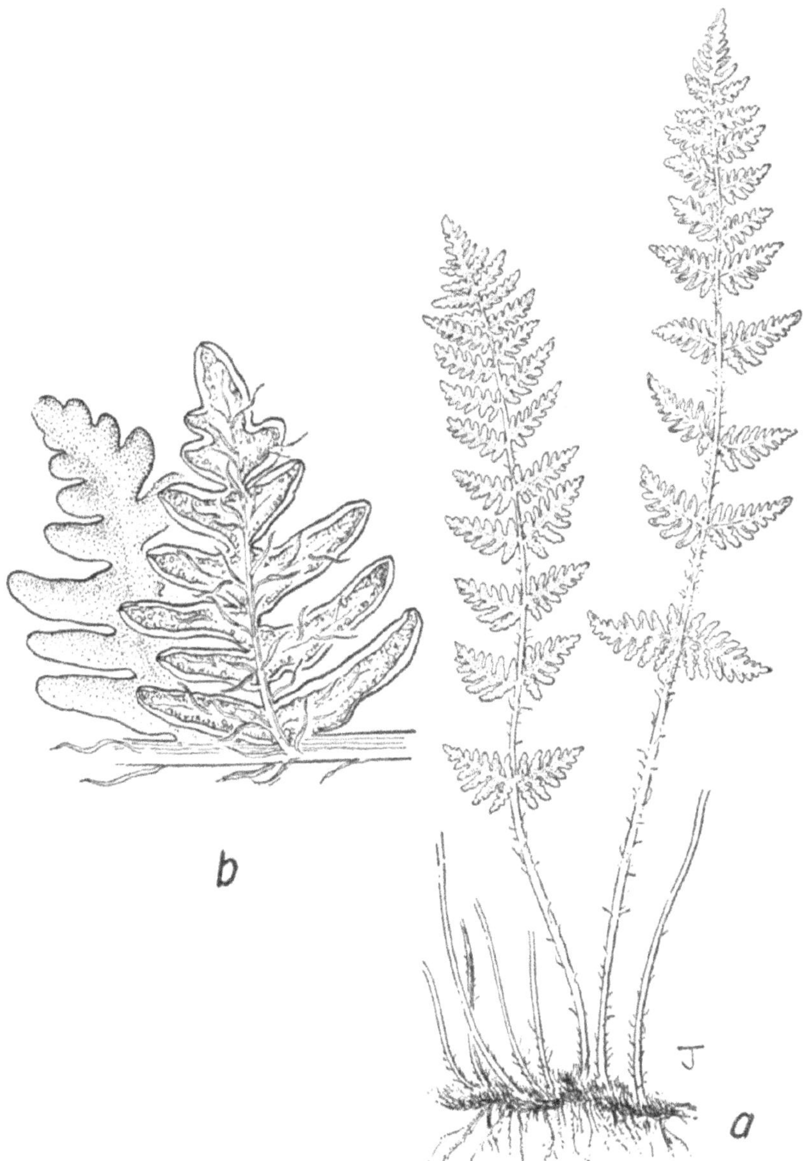

FIGURE 28. Notholaena Grayii. (a) habit × ¾, (b) views of upper and lower surfaces of pinnae × 3½.

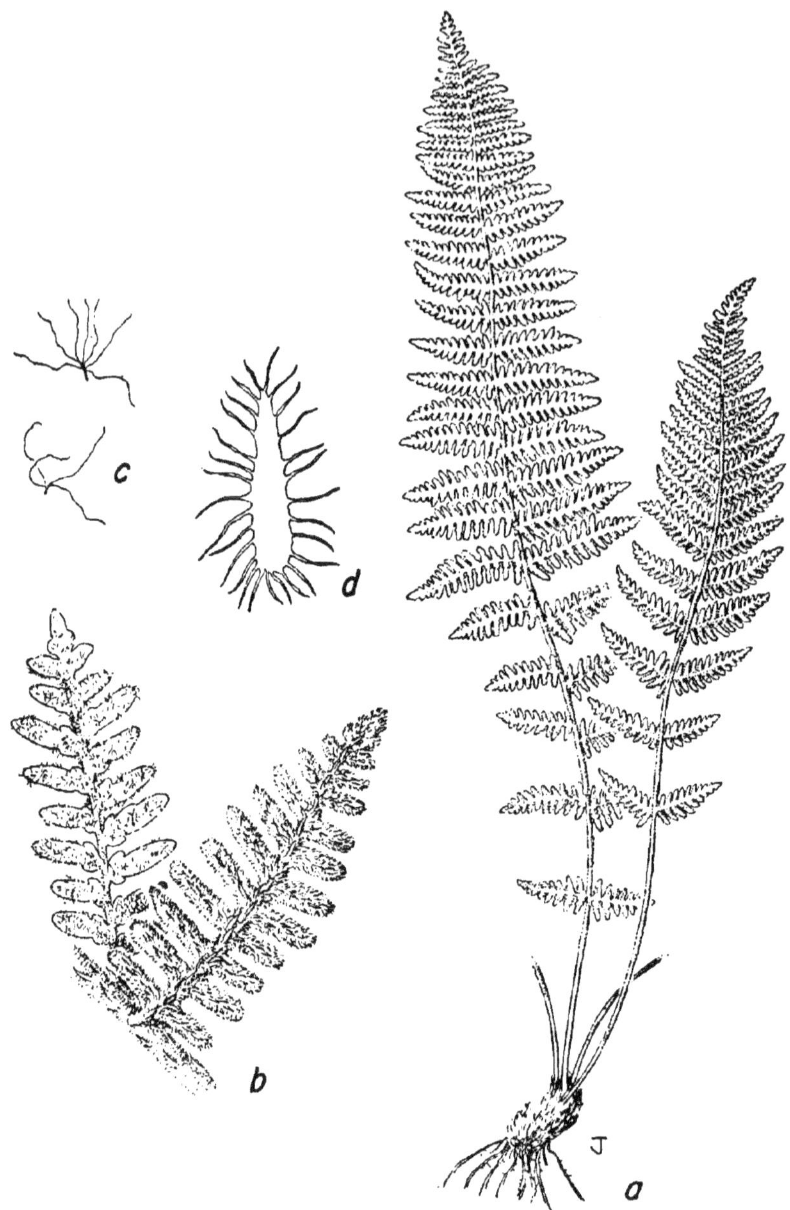

FIGURE 29. Notholaena Aschenborniana. (a) habit × ½, (b) views of upper and lower surfaces of pinnae × 3, (c) hairs from upper surface of pinnule × 17, (d) scale from lower surface of pinnule × 17.

Although we have seen no New Mexican specimens, the species has been collected close to the western border of New Mexico and it should be found within the state.

13. **CHEILANTHES** Lip Fern

Rhizomes short and suberect, or long-creeping, with abundant scales mostly having a dark central stripe; fronds uniform, once- to four-times pinnate, the ultimate pinnules often small, beadlike, woolly-pubescent or with chaffy scales, sometimes powdery; stipes dark, shiny, shorter than the blades; sori roundish, at the tip of the veins, numerous, often confluent; indusia false, formed by the recurved, whitish, more or less modified, often interrupted, sometimes membranaceous margins of the segments. The name is Greek in origin and means "margin flower," referring to the marginal sori.

A genus of mostly xerophytic low rock ferns comprising some 130 species over the temperate and tropical regions. The species are often difficult to separate.

Cheilanthes horridula Maxon is not listed in the "Key to the Species" although it possibly occurs in the state. There is in the United States National Herbarium a specimen of this species collected by the Mexican Boundary Survey under the number 1581 "near the Copper Mines and along the San Pedro." Standley[1] described the Copper Mines locality but made no mention of the San Pedro; and Wooton and Standley[2] reported this site as originally known as Santa Rita Del Cobre (now the town of Santa Rita), again making no mention of the San Pedro. It is thus presumed that Santa Rita is the site of the collection of specimen No. 1581, but one cannot be certain. Since the occurrence of the species in New Mexico is based upon this single collection, it seems advisable to await confirmation before definitely including it in the list of New Mexican species, particularly since it has not been listed by Morton[3] for adjacent Arizona. In the hope that students of ferns will search for the species in New Mexico, a description follows.

---

[1] Contributions from the United States National Herbarium 13: 170. 1910.

[2] *Flora of New Mexico.* Contributions from the United States National Herbarium 19: 769. 1915.

[3] Kearney and Peebles, *Arizona Flora.* Berkeley, 1915.

Cheilanthes horridula Maxon, Amer. Fern Journ. 8: 94. 1918. SPINOSE LIP FERN.

Rhizomes short, thick; fronds 5 inches long or less, bipinnate, the upper surfaces of the pinnae strongly scabrous owing to the numerous short, white, stiff spinulose hairs which arise at intervals from inflated conical bases in groups of 2 or 3; stipe slender, ebony-colored, bearing tawny scales; indusium broad, conspicuous.

Said to grow on rocky soils which have an alkaline reaction, this species is one of the rarest of the Mexican border ferns; it occurs in western Texas, Arbuckle Mountains of Oklahoma, Chihuahua, Coahuila, and Durango, and possibly in New Mexico and Arizona.

SYNONYMY

Cheilanthes aspera Hook., Sp. Fil. 2: 11. 1858, not Kaulf., 1831.
Pellaea aspera Baker in Hook. and Baker, Syn. Fil. 148. 1867.
Pellaea scabra C. Chr., Ind. Fil. 172. 1905.

KEY TO THE SPECIES

1. Rhizomes scarcely creeping, multicipital, erect or decumbent.

   2. Fronds devoid of scales, whitish-villous above, densely fulvous-tomentose beneath.....................................1. *C. Feei*

   2. Fronds scaly, at least on the stipe and rachis.

      3. Pinnae coarsely villous above; scales numerous beneath, closely imbricate, ovate, covering the whole under surface....2. *C. villosa*

      3. Pinnae tangled-hairy but not villous above, occasionally becoming glabrate in age, scaly along the rachis, the scales lanceolate to capillary, but not covering the whole under surface.

         4. Pinnae densely tomentose and gray above, densely matted-tomentose and tangled-woolly beneath; scales lanceolate.

3. *C. Eatonii*

         4. Pinnae arachnoid-villous and green above, loosely matted-tomentose, villous-tomentose, or glabrate in age beneath, the wool not tangled; scales on rachis very numerous, narrowly linear-subulate.....................................4. *C. tomentosa*

1. Rhizomes slender, creeping, or with elongated branches.

      5. Segments of pinnae minute, beadlike or rotund, often fan-shaped when young; fronds scaly, at least on the rachis.

         6. Pinnae closely tomentose above, the hairs entangling the segments............................5. *C. Lindheimeri*

6. Pinnae glabrous, or nearly so above, green, the hairs of adjacent segments not intertangled.

7. Scales widely imbricate on the lower surface of pinnae, wholly covering or exceeding the segments, long-ciliate at least at base......................6. *C. Wootonii*

7. Scales loosely imbricate along the veins, not covering the whole segment, not ciliate..........7. *C. Fendleri*

5. Segments of pinnae obtuse but not beadlike or rotund; pinnae without scales, glabrous to glabrate.

8. Stipes purplish-black, shiny, terete; indusia subcontinuous........................8. *C. alabamensis*

8. Stipes brown, dull, with a deep groove on upper side; indusia separate or nearly so.....9. *C. Wrightii*

1. **Cheilanthes Feei** Moore, Ind. Fil. 38. 1857. Fée's Lip Fern, Slender Lip Fern. (Figure 30.)

Rhizomes short, very scaly, the scales with a dark central stripe; fronds 2 to 8 inches long, densely tufted, slender, oblong-ovate, twice- to thrice-pinnate, the ultimate segments sometimes lobed, whitish-villous above, more densely dull yellow to brownish-tomentose beneath, becoming glabrate above in age; pinnae triangular, the crowded segments ovate, roundish, beadlike, the rachises scaleless; stipes about half the length of the frond, lustrous, dark purple, hairy, becoming somewhat glabrate in age; sori covering nearly the whole back of the pinnule, the recurved margin of which forms an almost continuous indusium.

A small fern of dry, rocky slopes or crevices of ledges, frequently on limestone. It ranges from Kentucky, Illinois, and Minnesota to British Columbia and Washington, and southward to southern California, Arizona, New Mexico, Missouri, Arkansas, Oklahoma, Texas, and northern Mexico.

New Mexico: Widely distributed in the mountain areas of the state. Organ, Tortugas, Burro, Guadalupe, Sacramento, White, San Andres, Socorro, Magdalena, Jemez, Sandia, Manzano, Taos, Santa Fe, and Las Vegas mountains; Black Range; Chaco Canyon; Llano Estacado; Ute Park; San Francisco River; 2 miles east of Folsom; Santa Rosa; Lakewood (Eddy County); Buchanan; Ice Caves and lava beds near Grants; Peña Blanca; 8 miles west of Reserve; lava beds just west of Carrizozo.

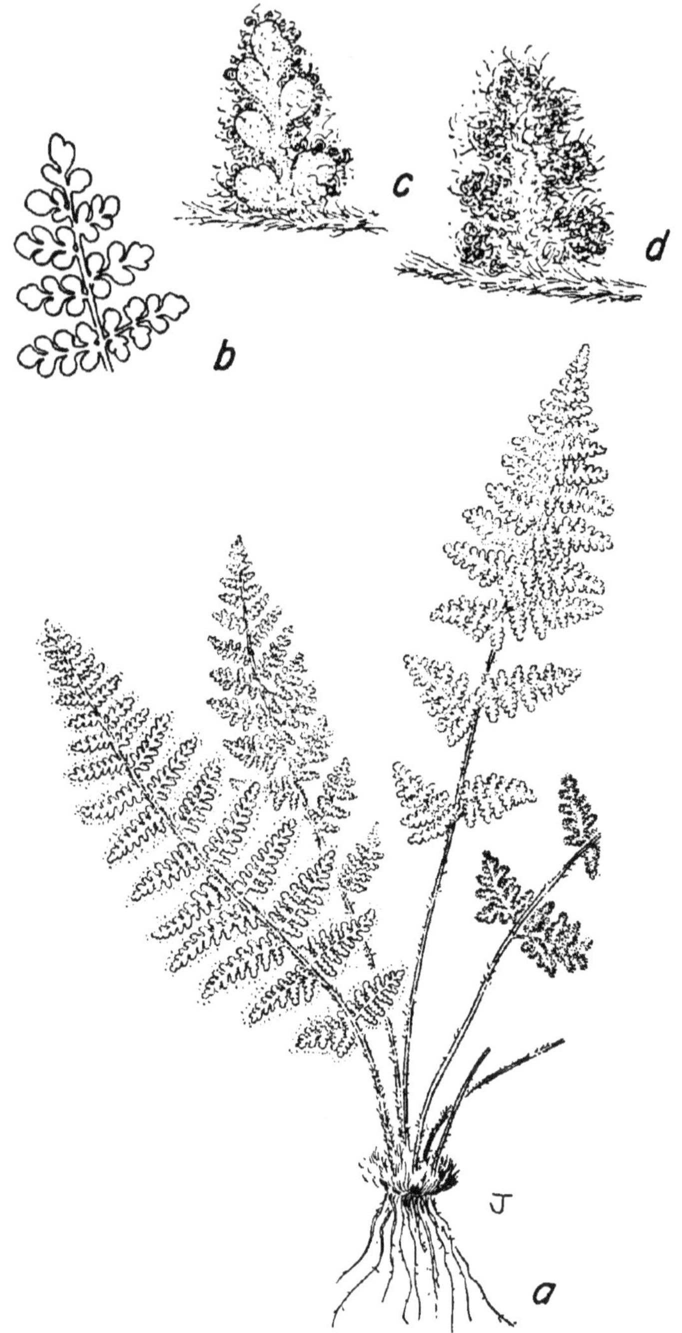

Figure 30. Cheilanthes Feei. (a) habit × ¾, (b) portion of pinna drawn without pubescence to show beaded shape of ultimate segments × 3½, (c) upper surface of pinnule × 7, (d) lower surface of pinnule showing sori × 7.

SYNONYMY

Cheilanthes gracilis Mett., Abhandl. Senckenb. Naturf. Gesell. 3: 80. 1859-61, not Kaulf., 1824.
Myriopteris gracilis Fée, Gen. Fil. 150. 1852.

2. Cheilanthes villosa Davenp. ex Maxon, Proc. Biol. Soc. Wash. 31: 142. 1918. (Figure 31.)

Rhizomes short, stout, bulblike, decumbent to suberect, multicipital, densely scaly, the long scales with a dark-brown median band in age; fronds numerous, erect, 4 to 8 inches long, narrowly lanceolate, tripinnatifid to tripinnate; pinnae mostly alternate, ascending, the lower ones somewhat remote; pinnules small, numerous, beadlike; blades coarsely villous or glabrate above in age, the hairs coarse, widely curved, flexuous and tortuous, densely scaly beneath, the erose-denticulate scales large, ovate, concealing the segments; stipes purplish-brown, usually half the length of the frond or less, with a nearly persistent covering of minute, appressed linear scales and numerous large, oblong, white or pale-tawny, spreading scales.

New Mexican specimens of *C. villosa* have often passed under the name *C. myriophylla* Desv. However, *C. myriophylla* is a Mexican and South American species which does not extend north of Mexico. *C. villosa* is a nearly related but well-defined species.

Found on granite or limestone ledges and slopes, it ranges from trans-Pecos Texas (Davis Mts.), southern New Mexico, and southern Arizona southward to Mexico and Guatemala.

New Mexico: Organ, Big Hatchet, Sacramento, San Andres, and Hanover mountains; Black Range.

3. Cheilanthes Eatonii Baker, in Hook. and Baker, Syn. Fil. 140. 1867. EATON'S LIP FERN. (Figure 32.)

Rhizomes short, thick; fronds many, broadly lanceolate, up to 12 inches in length, the lower pinnae somewhat remote; blades thrice-pinnate, the pinnae narrowly triangular; pinnules round to obovate and beadlike, tangled-densely tomentose and canescent above, brownish-tomentose beneath at maturity, the scales narrowly lanceolate, not concealing the segments; ultimate segments 1.5 to 2 mm. long with the rotund terminal

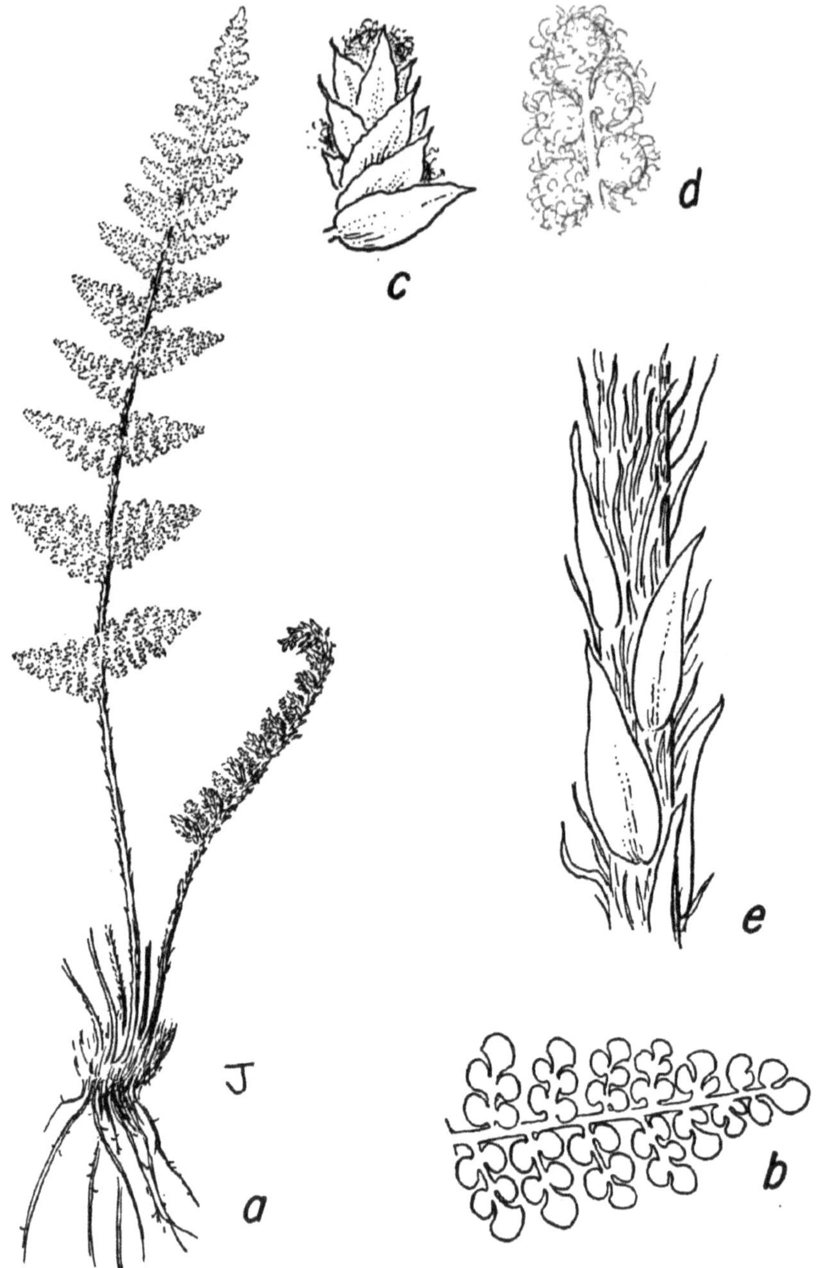

FIGURE 31. Cheilanthes villosa. (a) habit × ¾, (b) pinna drawn without pubescence to show beaded shape of ultimate segments × 8, (c) under surface of pinnule showing scales × 8, (d) upper surface of pinnule × 10, (e) portion of stipe × 12.

FIGURE 32. Cheilanthes Eatonii. (a) habit × ½, (b) pinna drawn without pubescence to show beaded shape of segments × 2½, (c) lower surface of pinnule × 10, (d) upper surface of pinnule × 5, (e) lower surface of pinnule showing marginal sori × 5, (f) portion of stipe × 6.

segment often larger; stipes brown, usually less than half the length of the blade, rather brittle, with long, narrow scales; sori small, practically hidden by the pubescence and the inrolled margins of the segments.

Plants with the upper surface of the blade green and sparingly villous are referable to f. *castanea* (Maxon) Correll (*Cheilanthes castanea* Maxon) .

Found at the base of ledges and on dry, rocky slopes, often on igneous rocks, it ranges from central Texas and western Oklahoma to Colorado, Utah, New Mexico, Arizona, and northern Mexico.

New Mexico: Organ, Dona Ana, San Andres, Guadalupe, White, Capitan, Big Hatchet, Burro, Tucumcari, Canyon, San Mateo, Socorro, San Luis, Mogollon, Magdalena, Hanover, Sandia, and Las Vegas mountains; Sierra Grande; Sangre de Cristo and Black ranges; Peña Blanca; Gray (Lincoln Co.); between Anton Chico and the mouth of Gallinas River; Romeroville; Ute Park; breaks of the Dry Cimarron River.

Synonymy

Cheilanthes castanea Maxon, Proc. Biol. Soc. Wash. 32: 111. 1919.
Cheilanthes Eatonii forma *castanea* (Maxon) Correll, Wrightia 1: 258. 1949.

4. Cheilanthes tomentosa Link, Hort. Berol. 2: 42. 1833. (Figure 33.)

Rhizomes short, erect, multicipital, densely scaly; fronds narrowly ovate-lanceolate, once- to thrice-pinnate, brown-woolly-pubescent below, usually green but sometimes hoary above; pinnules oblong to ovate; ultimate segments mostly less than 1 mm. in diameter; stipes usually less than half the length of the blade, slender with numerous flattened linear scales in addition to the hairs; sori almost hidden by the inrolled margin and pubescence.

Interestingly, *C. Eatonii* is often much more densely tomentose on the upper surface than is *C. tomentosa.*

Found in crevices of shady ledges or rocky slopes, it ranges from Virginia south to Georgia, westward to Arkansas, Oklahoma, Texas, New Mexico, Arizona, and northern Mexico.

New Mexico: Organ, Guadalupe, Las Vegas, Socorro, and Burro mountains; Black Range.

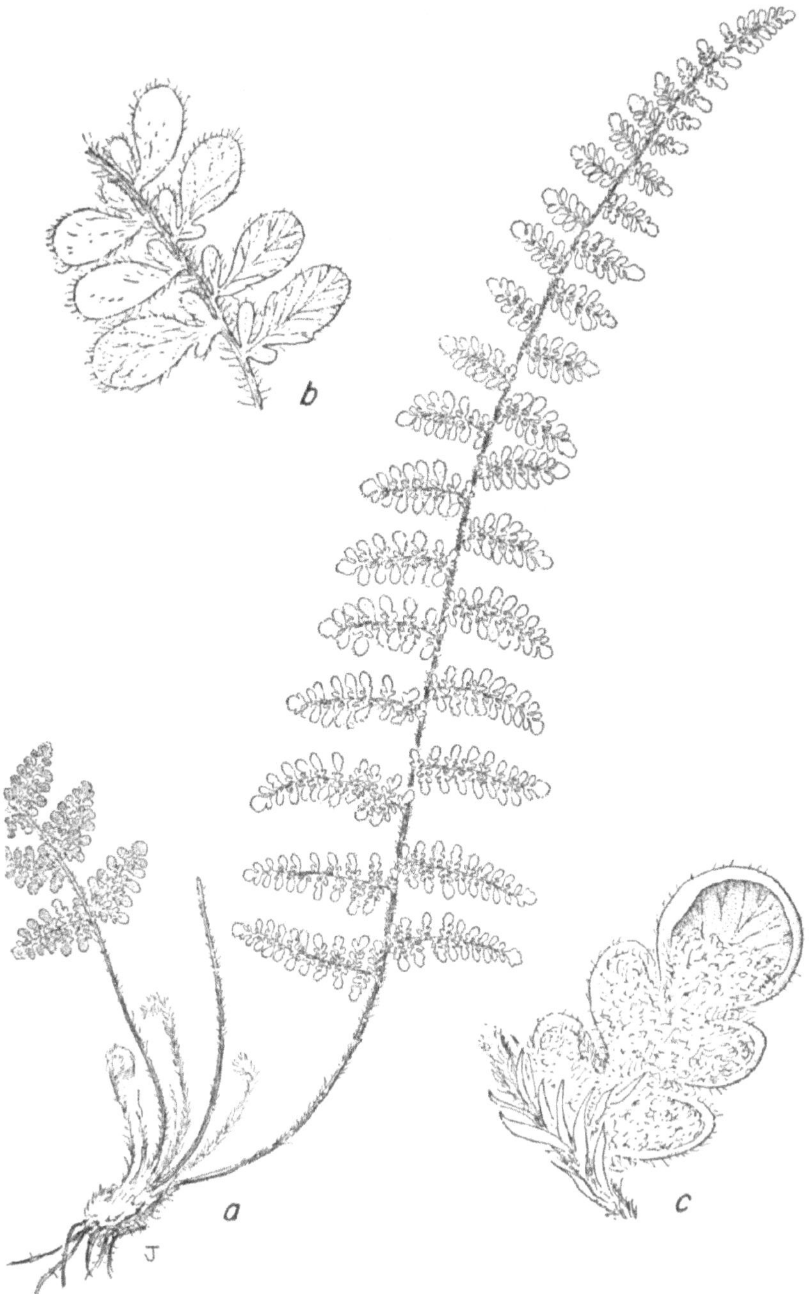

FIGURE 33. Cheilanthes tomentosa. (a) habit $\times$ 1/2, (b) upper surface of portion of pinna $\times$ 2½, (c) lower surface of pinnule $\times$ 5.

5. Cheilanthes Lindheimeri (J. Smith) Hook., Sp. Fil. 2: 101. 1858. (Figure 34.)

Rhizomes slender, creeping, much-branched, scaly; fronds 4 to 16 inches tall, narrowly ovate, twice- to thrice-pinnate, the ultimate segments thickish, beadlike, olive-green, white-tomentose above, the hairs entangling the adjacent pinnules, brown-hairy beneath; stipes scaly, about half the length of the frond; sori hidden by the pubescence and scales.

This species, rather large for the genus, is usually found on dry, igneous slopes. Apart from slight variation in size, it is remarkably constant throughout its range. It ranges from western Oklahoma through western Texas and westward to New Mexico, Arizona, and northern Mexico.

New Mexico: Organ, Dona Ana, Peña Blanca, Santa Rita, Burro, Telegraph, Tres Hermanas, and Florida mountains; Black Range.

SYNONYMY

Myriopteris Lindheimeri J. Smith in Seem., Bot. Voy. Herald 340. 1854.

6. Cheilanthes Wootonii Maxon, Proc. Biol. Soc. Wash. 31: 146. 1918. WOOTON'S LIP FERN. (Figure 35.)

Rhizomes slender, creeping, short-branched, scaly, the scales relatively broad, acutish to long-acuminate, mostly concolorous, persistent; fronds slender, narrowly oblong to lance-oblong, thrice-pinnate; pinnae mostly alternate, ascending, short-stalked, subequal in length; pinnules numerous, small, beadlike, glabrate above, grayish-white-scaly below when young, pale-brown-scaly pubescent when mature, the scales completely covering and extending beyond the ultimate segments, slender, attenuate to a hair-pointed, tortuous apex; stipes slender, sub-flexuous, chestnut-colored, mostly persistently scaly, the scales ascending, linear-attenuate to filiform; scales of the leaf rachises and ultimate segments numerous, ciliate at least in the basal part; sori concealed by the scales.

Found on dry ledges and banks, this species ranges from western Oklahoma, western Texas, and extreme southeastern Colorado southward to New Mexico, Arizona, and northern Mexico.

FIGURE 34. Cheilanthes Lindheimeri. (a) habit × ½, (b) pinna drawn without hairs showing beaded shape of ultimate segments × 3, (c) upper surface of pinnule × 6, (d) lower surface of pinnule × 6, (e) portion of stipe × 6.

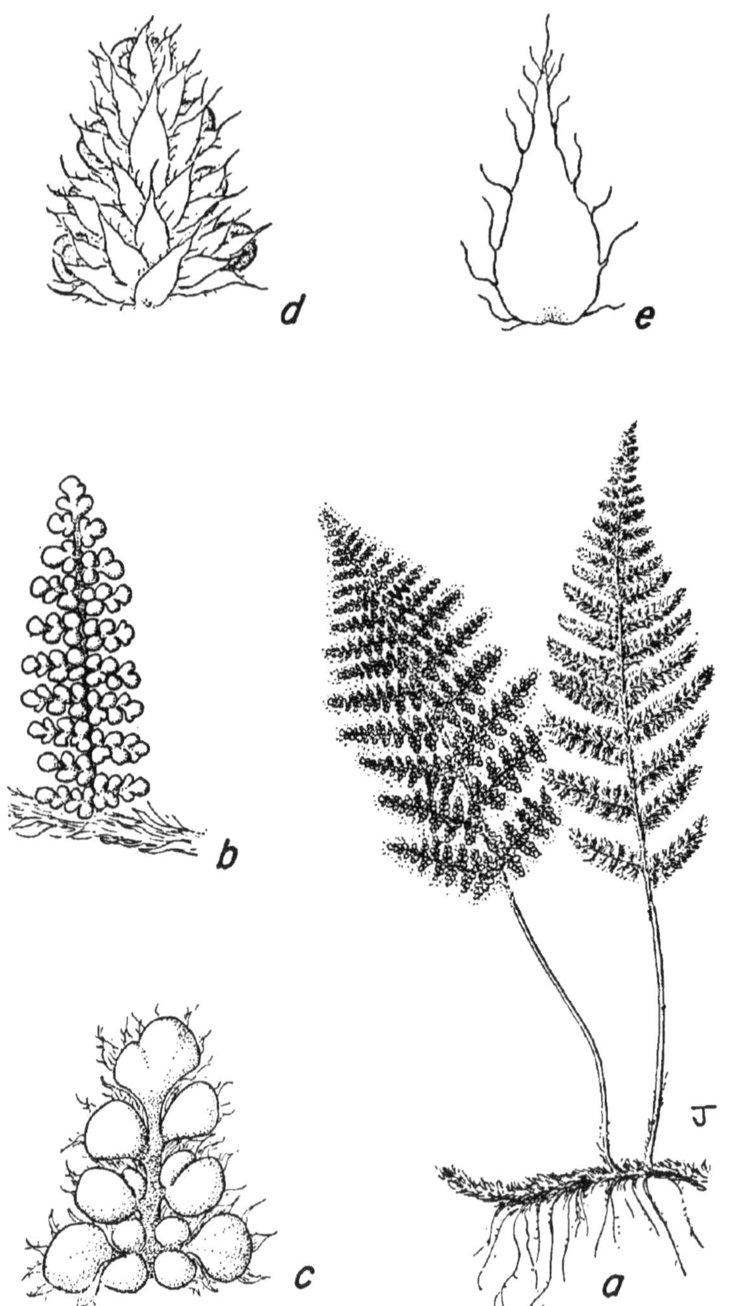

FIGURE 35. Cheilanthes Wootonii. (a) habit $\times$ 2/3, (b) pinna drawn without pubescence showing beaded shape of ultimate segments $\times$ 3½, (c) upper surface of pinnule $\times$ 7, (d) lower surface of pinnule $\times$ 10, (e) scale from lower surface of pinnule $\times$ 22.

New Mexico: Organ, Dona Ana, Florida, Santa Rita, Zuni, and Burro mountains; Black Range; breaks of the Dry Cimarron River.

7. Cheilanthes Fendleri Hook., Sp. Fil. 2: 103. 1858. FENDLER'S LIP FERN. (Figure 36.)

Rhizomes slender, branched, extensively creeping, coarse-scaly, the scales imbricate, narrowly ovate to long-attenuate, concolorous or nearly so, soon deciduous; fronds 3 to 12 inches tall, rather erect, broadly lanceolate, acuminate, thrice-pinnate; pinnae mostly alternate, oblique, the oblique pinnules variously lobed, somewhat beadlike, green and glabrous above, scaly along the midveins beneath, the scales not at all ciliate, not always covering the segments, long-attenuate, rather large, somewhat flexuous; stipes purplish-brown, ascending, nearly half as long as the frond, the light-brown scales linear-attenuate to filiform; sori partly hidden by the infolded segments.

Found on dry ledges, slopes, and cliffs, this species ranges from southern Colorado to Oklahoma and western Texas, westward to New Mexico, Arizona, and northern Mexico.

New Mexico: Organ, Dona Ana, Mimbres, Capitan, Big Burro, Burro, San Luis, Magdalena, Jemez, Manzano, Sandia, Santa Fe, and Las Vegas mountains; Sangre de Cristo and Black ranges; Sierra Grande; Folsom; Ute Park near Santa Rosa; breaks of the Dry Cimarron River; Romeroville.

In most of our mountains this species is frequently found growing with *C. Wootonii,* although *C. Fendleri* is more common and more widespread.

8. Cheilanthes alabamensis (Buckl.) Kunze, Linnaea 20: 4. 1847. ALABAMA LIP FERN. (Figure 37.)

Rhizomes widely creeping, branched, chaffy; fronds chartaceous, narrowly ovate-lanceolate, bipinnate, glabrous or slightly puberulent throughout, 4 to 12 inches tall, the divisions of the numerous oblong-lanceolate pinnae somewhat auricled or lobed; stipes slender, blackish, glabrous, scaleless except at base, about one-third the length of the frond; sori partly hidden by the nearly continuous, pale false indusium formed by the strongly recurved margin of the segments.

FIGURE 36. Cheilanthes Fendleri. (a) habit $\times$ ½, (b) pinna drawn without pubescence showing beaded shape of ultimate segments $\times$ 3, (c) upper surface of pinnule $\times$ 6, (d) lower surface of pinnule $\times$ 6, (e) scale from lower surface of pinnule $\times$ 18.

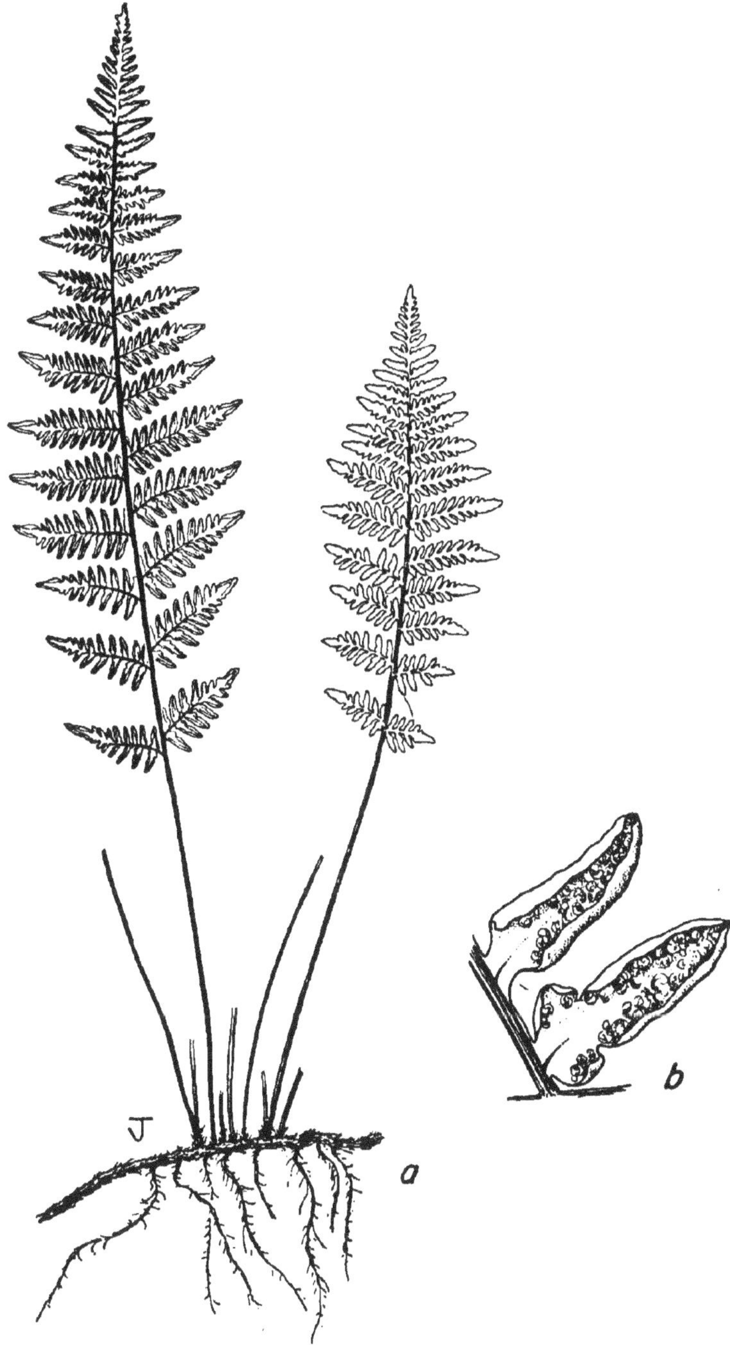

FIGURE 37. Cheilanthes alabamensis. (a) habit × ½, (b) lower surface of pinna × 6.

Not easily distinguished from *C. Wrightii* in the sterile state, but easily separated when indusia are present.

Found growing chiefly on calcareous cliffs and ledges, this species ranges from Virginia to Georgia, westward to Missouri, Oklahoma, Texas, southwestern New Mexico, southeastern Arizona, and northern Mexico; Jamaica.

New Mexico: Big Hatchet and Guadalupe mountains.

SYNONYMY

Pteris alabamensis Buckl., Amer. Journ. Sci. 45: 177. 1843.

9. Cheilanthes Wrightii Hook., Sp. Fil. 2: 87. 1858. WRIGHT'S LIP FERN. (Figure 38.)

Rhizomes slender, somewhat creeping; fronds narrowly to broadly lanceolate, bipinnate-pinnatifid to subtripinnate, divisions of pinnae variously lobed, crenate, or entire, glabrous to glabrate; stipes brown, dull, with a broad, deep ventral groove; rachises deeply channeled on the upper side; sori few, distinct, partly hidden by the infolded, irregularly indented, hyaline margins.

Found on igneous, sunny slopes and ledges, frequently with short grass, the species ranges from western Texas through southern New Mexico to southern Arizona and northern Mexico as far south as Durango. Rather generally distributed along the Mexican Border.

New Mexico: Bear and Telegraph mountains; Black Range.

14. CRYPTOGRAMMA ROCK BRAKE

Rhizomes short, suberect or somewhat creeping; fronds usually numerous, 3 to 12 inches long, strongly dimorphic; sterile fronds bi- to thrice-pinnatifid, markedly different in appearance from the fertile ones, being broader and shorter; fertile fronds bi- to rarely thrice-pinnatifid; sori roundish or elongated on the under side of the narrow pinnules and at first hidden by the infolded margin which expands at maturity exposing the sporangia. The name is derived from the Greek and means "hidden line," a reference to the line of sori which is hidden by the infolded margin of the pinnules.

A genus of five species, three in North America and two in Europe and Asia. Two of the North American species are

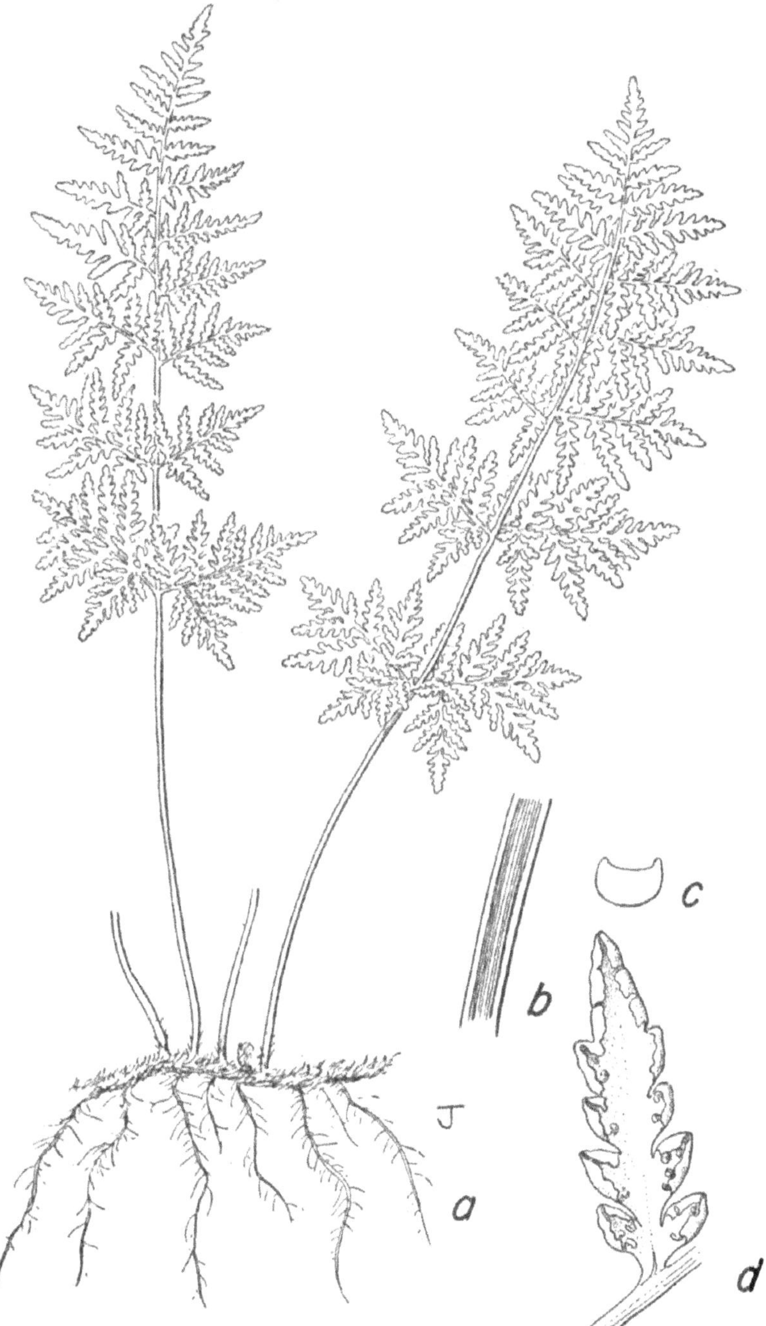

FIGURE 38. Cheilanthes Wrightii. (a) habit × ⅔, (b), (c) longitudinal and cross-sectional views of stipe showing deep ventral groove × 6, (d) lower surface of pinnule × 7.

reported from New Mexico; these are rather small plants of rocky situations.

KEY TO THE SPECIES

1. Fronds numerous, closely tufted from an erect or suberect rhizome.

1. *C. acrostichoides*

1. Fronds few, scattered along the creeping rhizome..........2. *C. Stelleri*

1. Cryptogramma acrostichoides R. Brown, in Richardson, Journ. Bot. App. Franklin, ed. 1, 754, 767. 1823. AMERICAN ROCK BRAKE. (Figure 39.)

Rhizomes short, suberect to erect, often in massive tufts; fronds numerous, bright green with pale stipes; sterile fronds bi- to thrice-pinnate or pinnatifid, 3 to 10 inches long, the pinnae papery to subcoriaceous, few, close, ovate-lanceolate; pinnules oblong to narrowly elliptic, crenate or slightly incised with rounded tips, glabrous; fertile fronds 4 to 12 inches long, surpassing the sterile ones, simpler with fewer segments, the fertile blades bi-, rarely thrice-pinnate or pinnatifid, the pinnules ¼ to ½ inch long, linear-oblong, the margins revolute at first, nearly meeting from the incurled sides and forming a false indusium which later expands releasing the spores; stipes deciduously scaly below, many of the basal scales with castaneous centers.

Growing on ledges and rocky hillsides, especially on rock slides, it ranges from Ontario to Alaska and southward to California, New Mexico, Colorado, Nebraska, and Michigan.

New Mexico: Found in the northern part of the state in Brazos Canyon, Rio Arriba County; Santa Fe and Las Vegas mountains; Sangre de Cristo Range.

SYNONYMY

Cryptogramma crispa var. *acrostichoides* (R. Brown) C. B. Clarke, Trans. Linn. Soc. London II, 1: 460. 1880.

2. Cryptogramma Stelleri (Gmel.) Prantl in Engler, Bot. Jahrb. 3: 413. 1882. SLENDER ROCK BRAKE, STELLER'S ROCK BRAKE. (Figure 40.)

Rhizomes creeping, slender, crisp, whitish; fronds few, scattered, 3 to 10 inches long, delicate; blades oblong-ovate to

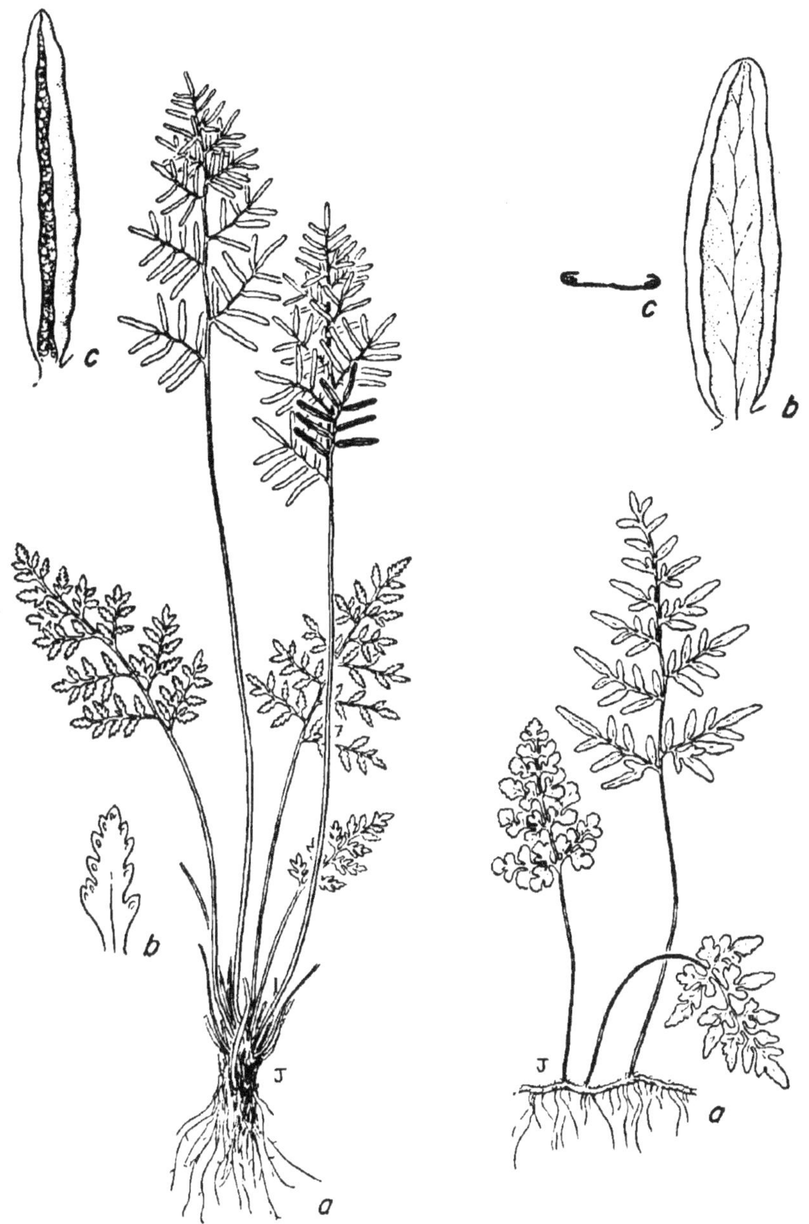

FIGURE 39. Cryptogramma acrostichoides. (a) plant showing sterile and fertile fronds × ½, (b) sterile pinnule × 3½, (c) lower surface of fertile pinnule × 7.

FIGURE 40. Cryptogramma Stelleri. (a) plant showing sterile and fertile fronds × ½, (b) lower surface of fertile pinnule × 8, (c) cross-section of fertile pinnule × 4.

lance-linear, pale or bright green, translucent when fresh, their fragile stipes almost scaleless, pale to purplish; sterile blades triangular-ovate, bipinnatifid or sometimes tripinnatifid, the pale green pinnae divided into wedge-shaped or fan-shaped segments, asymmetrical at base, the margins crenate or undulate; fertile blades stiffer, much longer than the sterile ones, with linear-oblong segments, the margins entire, occasionally somewhat hyaline; pinnule margins folded under, forming a false indusium.

Although this fern has a delicate appearance, it is actually quite hardy. It grows on moist, shady cliffs among calcareous rocks and on calcareous soils and is found especially in our northern states.

The species has been found in the mountains of northeastern Arizona just over our western border and has also been reported from just over the New Mexican border in southwestern Colorado. It is, therefore, very likely that it grows in the northern mountains of the state, but to date we have seen no specimen from New Mexico.

SYNONYMY

Pteris Stelleri Gmel., Nov. Comm. Acad. Sci. Petr. 12: 519. 1768.
Pellaea gracilis (Michx.) Hook., Sp. Fil. 2: 138. 1858.

15. ADIANTUM Maidenhair Fern

Delicate, graceful plants of moist ledges, ravines, or rocky woods. Rhizomes scaly, widely creeping or thick and suberect; fronds ascending or drooping, with black or red-black, lustrous stipes and rachises; blades membranaceous, once- to bi-, rarely thrice-pinnate, the pinnae in 2 vertical ranks, extremely variable according to fertility of soil; sori elongate on the veins on the under side of reflexed, marginal, indusiumlike lobes.

A genus of about 200 species. Some of the handsomest and most delicate ferns are found in this group. The name is from the Greek meaning "unwet," an allusion to the fact that the pinnae repel raindrops. A single species is found in our range.

1. **Adiantum Capillus-Veneris** L., Sp. Pl. 1096. 1753. Venus' Hair, Southern Maidenhair. (Figure 41.)

Rhizomes creeping, slender, covered with light-brown, chaffy scales; fronds numerous, ovate-lanceolate, up to 24 inches long,

FIGURE 41. Adiantum Capillus-Veneris. (a) habit × ½, (b) lower surface of pinnule × 1, (c) sorus × 5.

mostly bi-, occasionally thrice-pinnate below, once-pinnate above, laxly ascending or drooping; blades generally light green, rather long-stiped; pinnules stalked, obliquely fan-shaped to rhomboid, deeply lobed or deeply incised on the outer margins, serrate; stipes and rachises polished, slender, blackish-purple.

Palmer reports that in Mexico this plant is sold in the market in Saltillo "to assist in the menstruations in females." In some parts of the United States it is used in making sprays and wreaths for funeral decorations.

Found on moist, usually limestone ledges, cliffs or wet, rocky banks. Wet ledges are frequently densely festooned with the pendant fronds of this beautiful fern. It is widely distributed especially in the warmer parts of both hemispheres. British Columbia, South Dakota, and Virginia, south to Florida and westward to Kentucky, Tennessee, Missouri, Oklahoma, Texas, New Mexico, Colorado, Utah, Arizona, and California; northwestern Mexico; Old World. The name *Capillus-Veneris* means "Venus' hair."

The New Mexican plants have been referred to var. *modestum* (Underw.) Fernald, which differs only slightly from the typical variety. The type came from North Spring River, Roswell, New Mexico (Earle 261).

New Mexico: Sangre de Cristo and Black ranges; Ash Canyon in San Andres, Mogollon, Guadalupe, Sacramento, and Sandia mountains; Blue Hole at Santa Rosa; Spring River, Roswell; Black River, Eddy County; 8 miles northwest of Reserve.

Synonymy

Adiantum modestum Underw., Bull. Torr. Bot. Club 28: 46. 1901.
Adiantum rimicola Slosson, Bull. Torr. Bot. Club 41: 308. 1914.
Adiantum Capillus-Veneris var. *modestum* Fernald, Rhodora 52: 206. 1950.

16. PTERIDIUM Bracken Fern

Coarse ferns of almost world-wide distribution; rhizomes widely creeping, deeply underground, cordlike; fronds large, 8 to 48 inches tall, quite variable, ranging from bipinnate to tripinnatifid or tripinnate, the ultimate segments themselves sometimes lobed, leathery, the lower pinnae with basal nectaries; pinnae of the primary rachis opposite or nearly so, other divisions alternate or nearly so, the margins revolute; stipe half as long as the blade or shorter; sori marginal on the upper pinnae of the fronds, continuous in age, the whole margin of the pinnae reflexed and continuous, forming a false indusium.

A genus of a single cosmopolitan species with many geographical subspecies. The name is from the Greek, a diminutive of *pteris,* signifying "little fern."

1. **Pteridium aquilinum** (L.) Kuhn, in V. Decken, Reisen in Ost-Afrika 3, pt. 3: 11. 1879. BRAKE, BRACKEN, or EAGLE FERN. (Figure 42.)

Rhizomes hairy, coarse, thick, spreading, often 3 feet long or more and sometimes deep beneath the surface of the ground; fronds bi- to thrice-pinnate, erect; pinnules variable in shape in our specimens, ranging from narrowly lanceolate to ovate or deltoid with distinct lobes at the base of some of the pinnules; sori marginal, borne on a receptacle connecting the ends of the veins, covered when young with a thin, somewhat indefinite, minute inner indusium and with an outer false indusium formed by the reflexed margins of the segments.

Almost world-wide in distribution, this coarse fern is very abundant on the North American continent.

The New Mexican plant is *P. aquilinum* var. *pubescens* Underw., which is widely distributed in western and northern North America. Our specimens vary considerably as to pubescence, which sometimes covers the whole under side of the pinnules, sometimes occurs only on the lower side of the mid-veins, or is nearly lacking.

New Mexico: White, Capitan, Sacramento, Mogollon, San Luis, Tunitcha, Pinos Altos, Sandia, Jemez, Santa Fe, and Las Vegas mountains; Mt. Taylor, Sangre de Cristo and Black ranges; Ice Caves near Grants. Abundant in meadows and at the upper levels of the yellow pine and lower levels of the Douglas fir-aspen as well as spruce associations. As an example, in the western portion of the Mogollon Mountains this species covers entire hillsides as an undergrowth among the dominant yellow pine. Moreover, it becomes established in over-grazed meadows.

FIGURE 42. Pteridium aquilinum var. pubescens. (a) frond $\times$ ½, (b) lower surface of pinnule $\times$ 2, (c) greatly enlarged cross-section of margin of pinnule showing sporangia.

This fern is reported to be poisonous to horses and cattle when eaten in large quantities, although the poisonous element may be destroyed by cooking. The rhizomes and young fronds are sometimes utilized for human food.

SYNONYMY

Pteris aquilina L., Sp. Pl. 1075. 1753.
Pteridium aquilinum var. *pubescens* Underw., Our Nat. Ferns, ed. 6, 91. 1900.

17. **POLYPODIUM** POLYPODY

Shade-loving ferns of various habitats, commonly growing among rocks or epiphytic on trees. Rhizomes branched, widely creeping, often covered with chaffy scales; fronds uniform, attached near the bases of the stipes by distinct articulations to knoblike prominences on the rhizome; blades glabrous or pubescent, often evergreen and somewhat leathery, simple but deeply pinnatifid, the segments entire or merely denticulate, usually alternate; sori large and round, located on or at the ends of the veins, lacking indusia from the beginning.

A genus of about 75 mostly epiphytic species mainly confined to tropical and subtropical America, Asia, and Polynesia. About 8 species have been reported from the United States, one of which definitely, the other probably, is found in New Mexico. The name is from the Greek, meaning "many feet," an allusion to the knoblike prominences on the rhizome.

KEY TO THE SPECIES

1. Stipes and lower surfaces of blades scaleless; segments remotely toothed; rhizome scales concolorous; veins obvious, all free.........1. *P. vulgare*

1. Stipes and lower surfaces of blades densely scaly; segments entire; rhizome scales with a dark median band; veins obscure, partly anastomosing.
2. *P. thyssanolepis*

1. **Polypodium vulgare** L., Sp. Pl. 1085. 1753. WESTERN POLYPODY. (Figure 43.)

Terrestrial plants; rhizomes creeping, densely scaly, rather sweet to the taste; fronds 3 to 10 inches long, blades ovate-oblong, deeply pinnatifid, the lobes oblong, obtuse, usually alternate, the edges shallowly serrate to nearly entire; stipes straw-colored, rather long, sometimes as long as the blade,

FIGURE 43. Polypodium vulgare. (a) habit × 1, (b) lower surface of pinnule × 4½.

grooved on the upper side, articulate near the base; sori borne on each side of the midvein midway between the vein and the margin.

This plant grows on cliffs and rocky slopes and is widely distributed in North America and Eurasia. In North America it extends from Canada to Mexico.

The New Mexican collections are *P. vulgare* L. var. *columbianum* Gilbert (*P. hesperium* Maxon, *P. prolongilobum* Clute, *P. vulgare* var. *perpusillum* Clute) .

New Mexico: Vicinity of Brazos Canyon in Rio Arriba County; Sandia Mountains.

SYNONYMY

Polypodium hesperium Maxon, Proc. Biol. Soc. Wash. 13: 200. 1900.
Polypodium vulgare var. *columbianum* Gilbert, List No. Amer. Pterid. 19, 38. 1901.

2. **Polypodium thyssanolepis** A. Braun ex Klotzsch, Linnaea 20: 392. 1847.

A rock fern with widely creeping, scaly rhizomes, the scales with a dark median band; fronds ovate, subcoriaceous, the segments entire and densely scaly beneath; stipe bearing two furrows, densely scaly.

Said to grow among rocks in canyons and on rocky hillsides, it ranges from western Texas to southeastern Arizona; West Indies; Mexico to Peru.

Tidestrom and Kittell[1] by inference have included New Mexico within the range of this species, and since it grows in Texas and Arizona it may occur in New Mexico as well. However, to date we have seen no specimen collected in New Mexico.

II. OPHIOGLOSSACEAE ADDER'S TONGUE FAMILY

Terrestrial, rarely epiphytic, herbs; rhizomes short, erect, fleshy, glabrous and scaleless, bearing enlarged, hairless mycorrhizal roots; fronds scaleless, erect (not circinate) in vernation, consisting of a simple, erect, fleshy stipe enlarged at the base and upwardly bearing sterile and fertile structures; fertile portions spikelike or paniculate, markedly unlike the sterile; sterile

---

[1] *A Flora of Arizona and New Mexico*, Washington, 1941, p. 877.

portion green, simple or compound, arising laterally; sporangia marginal in 2 rows, large, globose; spores numerous, thick-walled, all alike, yellow; prothallia small, subterranean, usually devoid of chlorophyll.

A small family of three genera, the 53 species widely distributed throughout the world.

KEY TO THE GENERA

1. Sterile blades mostly lobed or compound with free veins; fertile portion paniculate...1. *Botrychium*

1. Sterile blades simple with anastomosing veins; fertile portion spicate.
2. *Ophioglossum*

1. **BOTRYCHIUM** Grape Fern, Moonwort

Succulent terrestrial plants with stout, erect rhizomes bearing clustered, fleshy roots and mostly solitary fronds with a short common stalk, the sterile blades sessile or stalked, pinnately to subpalmately compound, the segments often much divided, glabrous or pubescent with simple hairs; fertile portion long, paniculately branched, the divisions bearing double rows of sporangia.

This genus comprises 23 widely distributed species, somewhat diversified as to size and nature of the sterile frond, and found mostly in the Arctic and Northern Temperate Zones, a few in the Tropics and Antarctic. The name is Greek in origin and signifies "a bunch of grapes," an allusion to the fertile portion of the frond.

KEY TO THE SPECIES

1. Buds (inside base of stalk) hairy; sterile blades usually more than 2½ inches long...1. *B. multifidum*

1. Buds glabrous; sterile blades mostly less than 2½ inches long.

  2. Sterile blades inserted well above the middle of the plant, usually bipinnatifid to bipinnate, the ultimate segments narrow, oblong.
2. *B. lanceolatum*

  2. Sterile blades inserted at or below the middle of the plant, simple to pinnate, the ultimate segments often fan-shaped.

    3. Sterile blades short-petioled, arising near the base of the plant.
3. *B. simplex*

    3. Sterile blades sessile, arising near the middle of the plant.
4. *B. Lunaria*

1. **Botrychium multifidum** ssp. **Coulteri** (Underw.) Clausen, Mem. Torr. Bot. Club 19: 36. 1938. BROADLEAF GRAPE FERN.

Plants stout and decidedly fleshy, 6 to 9 inches tall with many fleshy roots; buds hairy; sterile blade stalk ½ to 2 inches long inserted near the base of the plant, the blade usually triparted, each division tripinnatifid to quadripinnatifid, the segments obliquely ovate, the margin entire or slightly wavy; sporophyll large, paniculate.

This subspecies is known only from scattered localities in Washington, Oregon, California, and possibly Colorado.

Although no collections have been reported for New Mexico there is reason to believe that this species will be found within the state.

SYNONYMY

Botrychium Coulteri Underw., Bull. Torr. Bot. Club 25: 537. 1898.

2. **Botrychium lanceolatum** (Gmel.) Angstr., ssp. **typicum** Clausen, Mem. Torr. Bot. Club 19: 90. 1938. LANCELEAVED GRAPE FERN. (Figure 44.)

Plants somewhat succulent, 2 to 12 inches tall; sterile blade sessile or nearly so, attached near the top of the common stalk, triangular or deltoid, once- to twice-pinnate or -pinnatifid, the segments oblique, oblong-lanceolate, entire, incised or toothed; fertile spikes short-stalked, paniculate, bi- to thrice-pinnate, mostly extending above the sterile blade.

A plant of the subarctic and arctic-alpine floras, it is found in a variety of habitats, including dry slopes, alpine meadows, sandy open places, and even swampy forests. This variety ranges in the northeast from Greenland, Newfoundland, and Quebec south to northern Maine; in the northwest it occurs from the Aleutian Islands southward through British Columbia to Washington, Wyoming, and Colorado. It is also found in Scotland, Scandinavia, France, Switzerland, Austria, Finland, Russia, Siberia, and Japan. In the western United States this subspecies is quite variable.

Although no specimens have been collected in New Mexico, it is reasonable to expect it to be found within the state.

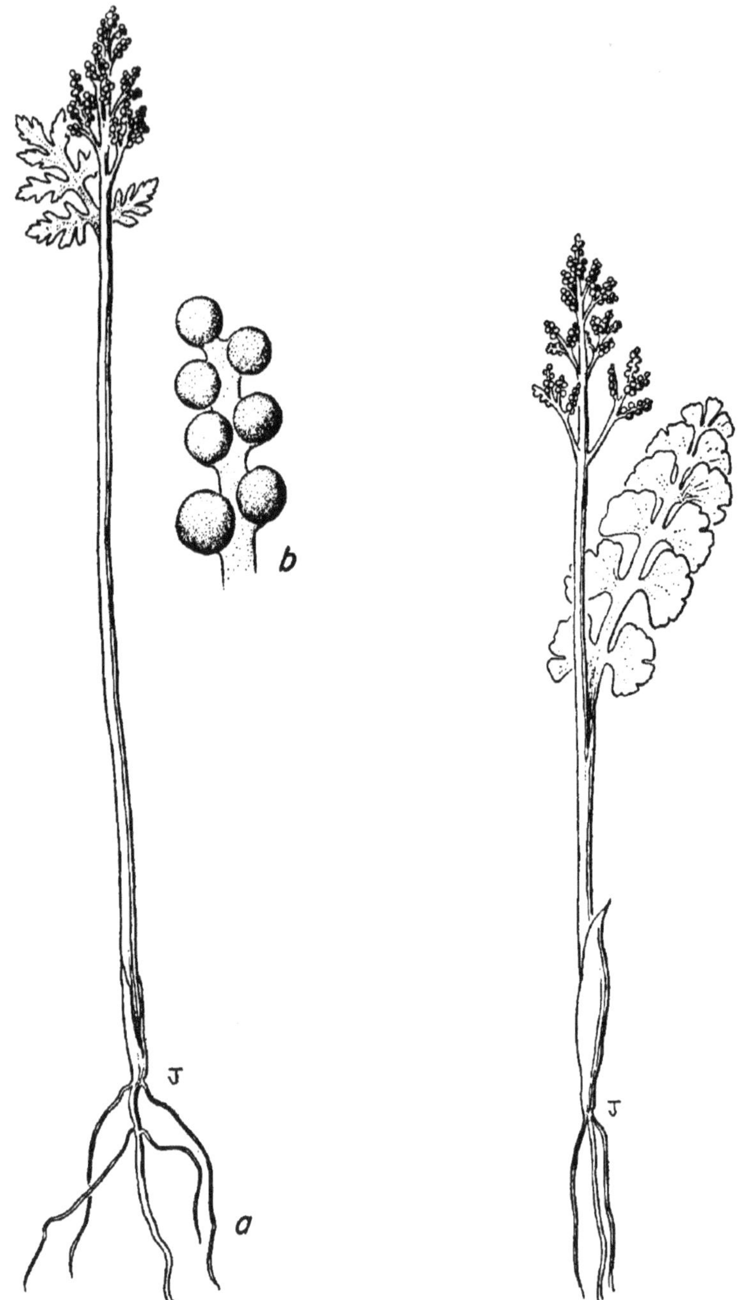

FIGURE 44. Botrychium lanceolatum ssp. typicum. (a) plant showing sterile blade and fertile spike × ½, (b) double row of sporangia × 6.

FIGURE 45. Botrychium Lunaria. Plant showing sterile blade and fertile spike × ½.

Osmunda lanceolata Gmel., Nov. Comment. Acad. Petrop. 12: 516. 1768.
Botrychium lanceolatum (Gmel.) Angstr., Bot. Notiser. Nos. 5 and 6: 68. 1854.

3. Botrychium simplex E. Hitch. var. typicum Clausen, Mem. Torr. Bot. Club 19: 70-74. 1938. LITTLE GRAPE FERN.

Plants stout, straight, smooth, fleshy, 2 to 10 inches tall; bud glabrous with both fertile and sterile segments erect or with tip of sterile slightly inclined over the fertile; sterile blade subsessile, arising near the base of the common stalk, simple, lobed, or pinnately divided, the divisions oblong, rhomboid, or kidney-shaped, usually overlapping, the basal divisions again divided; fertile portion a simple or compound spike.

This species, a plant of open spaces growing in pastures and meadows and on shores and gravelly slopes, is distributed from Newfoundland, Nova Scotia, and Quebec south to Massachusetts, New York, and Pennsylvania; westward to Ontario, Wisconsin, and British Columbia; and southward through Oregon and Montana to Colorado, New Mexico, and California; Northern Europe; Corsica; Japan.

New Mexico: Santa Fe Creek Valley, Santa Fe, A. Fendler 1014.

Botrychium simplex E. Hitch., Amer. Journ. Sci. 6: 103. 1823.

4. Botrychium Lunaria (L.) Swartz, Schrad. Journ. Bot. 2: 110. 1800. MOONWORT. (Figure 45.)

Plants fleshy, 2 to 10 inches tall, straight; sterile blade subsessile, arising near the middle of the plant, once-pinnate, the segments fan-shaped to lunate or kidney-shaped, and varying from crenate to entire, often overlapping; fertile portion paniculate, bi- to thrice-pinnate.

Found in meadows, on slopes and banks, as well as in woods. It ranges throughout northern Europe; Asia, where it extends southward to northern India; and boreal North America, where it is distributed from Newfoundland to Alaska and southward to Maine, Michigan, and Minnesota, and through the Rocky Mountains to California, Colorado, Arizona, and possibly New Mexico.

Since no specimens have been found in the state, it is not possible to designate the variety.

Osmunda Lunaria L., Sp. Pl. 1064. 1753.

2. OPHIOGLOSSUM ADDER'S TONGUE

A genus of 28 species spread throughout the globe; generally small terrestrial plants with small, often tuberous rhizomes, the tropical species sometimes large epiphytes; leaves 1 or 2, glabrous, the stipe green; blades divided into a simple, entire, elliptic sterile blade and an erect, simple fertile spike bearing two rows of sporangia near the summit, the entire sporophyll green when immature, brown at maturity. The name is from the Greek and means "serpent tongue."

1. **Ophioglossum Engelmannii** Prantl, Ber. Deut. Bot. Gesell. 1: 351. 1883. ADDER'S TONGUE.

Rhizome short, oblique, tuberlike, with several naked branches; fronds divided into two parts, one of which is usually sterile, 2 to 5 inches long, ovate-lanceolate, entire, somewhat fleshy, yellow-green, usually attached well below the middle; fertile stalk as long or longer than the common stalk.

A species of limestone regions, being found especially in clayey depressions between limestone ledges, in clay barrens, in pastures, in open and grassy woodlands, and also in cedar barrens and glades. It ranges from northwestern Virginia westward through southern Ohio and Illinois to Missouri, and southward to central Florida, Louisiana, Texas, Oklahoma, Arizona, and central and southern Mexico.

Although no specimen of this plant has been reported from New Mexico there is reason to believe that it should be found in the state.

III. MARSILEACEAE PEPPERWORT FAMILY

1. MARSILEA

This genus is a remnant of an ancient family that today comprises only 3 genera and about 70 species. *Marsilea,* consisting of about 65 species, is found in shallow, stagnant water or muddy flats in temperate and tropical regions of the world but most commonly in Australia and South Africa. Named in honor of Fernando Conte Marsigli, an Italian naturalist of the late 17th and early 18th centuries.

1. Marsilea mucronata A. Br., Amer. Journ. Sci. II 3: 55. 1847. PEPPERWORT. (Figure 46.)

Aquatic or subaquatic, herbaceous perennials with long-creeping, much-branched, slender rhizomes, these hairy and rooting at the nodes; leaves alternate in two rows, coiled in the bud, each of the long stipes bearing a four-foliate, cloverlike leaf, folding upward at night; sporocarps green, solitary, bony, rather large, ovoid, each with 2 tubercles, vertically two-valved, and borne on short stalks at the base of the stipe; sori several within the sporocarp, in 2 rows, each sorus surrounded by a delicate indusium and bearing both megaspores and micro-spores, the megaspores producing prothallia bearing archegonia and the microspores producing prothallia bearing antheridia, both prothallia being small.

We follow Mr. C. A. Weatherby (Journ. Arnold Arbor. 24: 325. 1943) in maintaining *M. mucronata* as a species distinct from *M. vestita*. The two are more or less geographically distinct, *M. vestita* being restricted to the Pacific coast, and *M. mucronata* to the high plains, Rocky Mountains, and southwestern states. The greater abundance of long, slender, somewhat spreading hairs distinguishes *M. vestita,* those of *M. mucronata* being sparser, shorter, broader, and more strongly appressed.

M. mucronata ranges from southern Saskatchewan and Alberta south to Oklahoma, Texas, New Mexico, and Arizona.

New Mexico: Ponds near Las Vegas, temporary ponds near Queen in Eddy County; 4 miles southeast of Clines Corners. Undoubtedly it may be found in other places in the state, especially along our eastern border.

IV. SALVINIACEAE WATER FERN FAMILY

Small, free-floating plants; rhizomes threadlike, branched; leaves small, green or purplish, alternating in 2 rows along the branched axis; plants monoecious, the sporocarps borne terminally in pairs on the lower submersed leaf lobe.

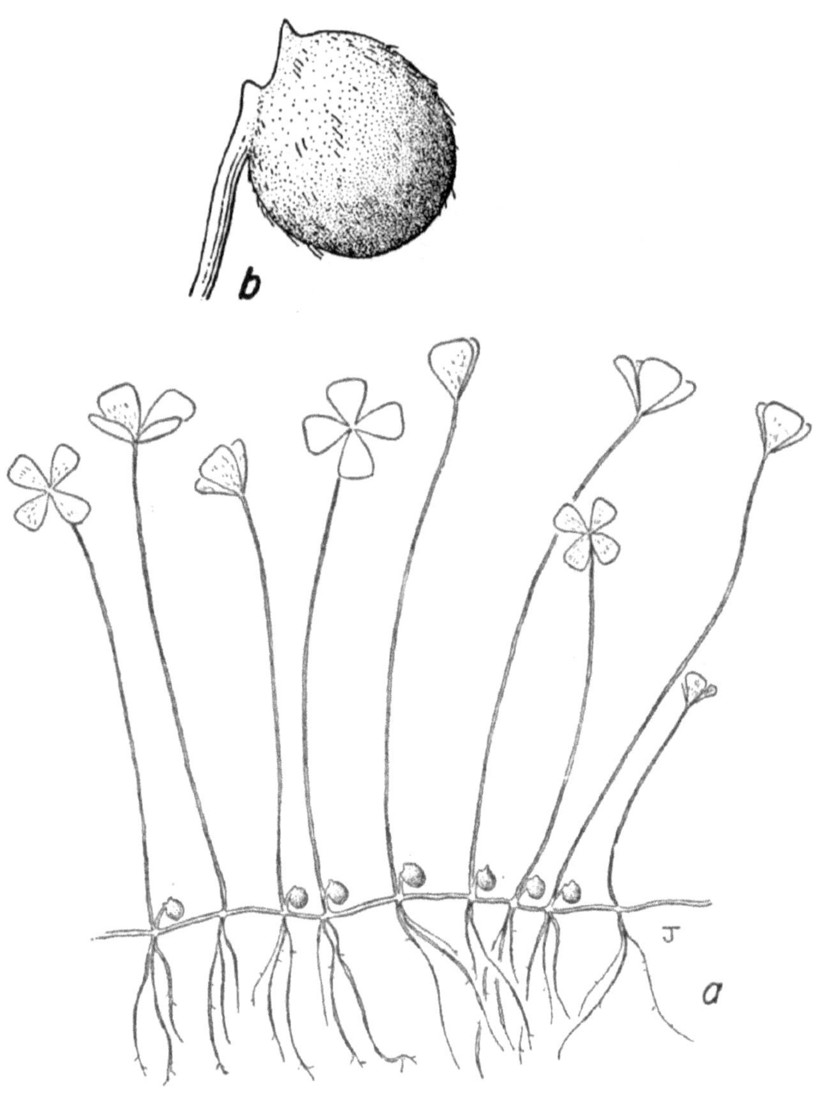

FIGURE 46. Marsilea mucronata. (a) habit × ⅔, (b) sporocarp × 6.

A small family of plants not closely related to other groups of the Pteridophyta. Generally found in stagnant or still water especially along drainage ditches.

1. **AZOLLA** Mosquito Fern

A small genus of 6 species found chiefly in the tropics. The very small plants somewhat deltoid in outline, with elongated, branching stems and slender, unbranched roots, the stems bearing small, papillose leaves (about 2 mm. in diameter) with two ovate lobes; sporocarps terminal on the leaf lobes, the indusium forming the thin sporocarp wall; sporocarps soft, 2 or more on a stalk, each acorn-shaped megasporangium containing a single megaspore, each globular microsporangium bearing numerous microspores. Both kinds of spores produce small prothallia. The name *Azolla* is a combination of two Greek words meaning "to dry" and "to destroy," which might be more fittingly stated as "killed by drought."

1. **Azolla mexicana** Presl, Abh. Böhm. Ges. Wiss. 3: 150. 1845. (Figure 47.)

This is the only species found in our range. It grows very abundantly on lake and pond waters and in the clear, quiet waters of large irrigation ditches; although it grows most abundantly in summer, it can be found throughout the year. The plant is most readily recognized by its purplish color and surface growth wherever it is found. It may at times be mistaken for a tiny seed-plant, duckweed *(Lemna)*, with which it often grows. The species is characterized by many-septate glochidia, dichotomously branched plants with the lower leaf lobes much longer than the upper ones, microsporangia which usually bear 4 massulae, and pitted megaspores.

This species occurs in Mexico and has a scattered distribution in the lowlands southward to French Guiana and Bolivia, northward to Utah and British Columbia, and eastward to Wisconsin and Illinois.

New Mexico: Widely distributed in the state, common in the Rio Grande Valley.

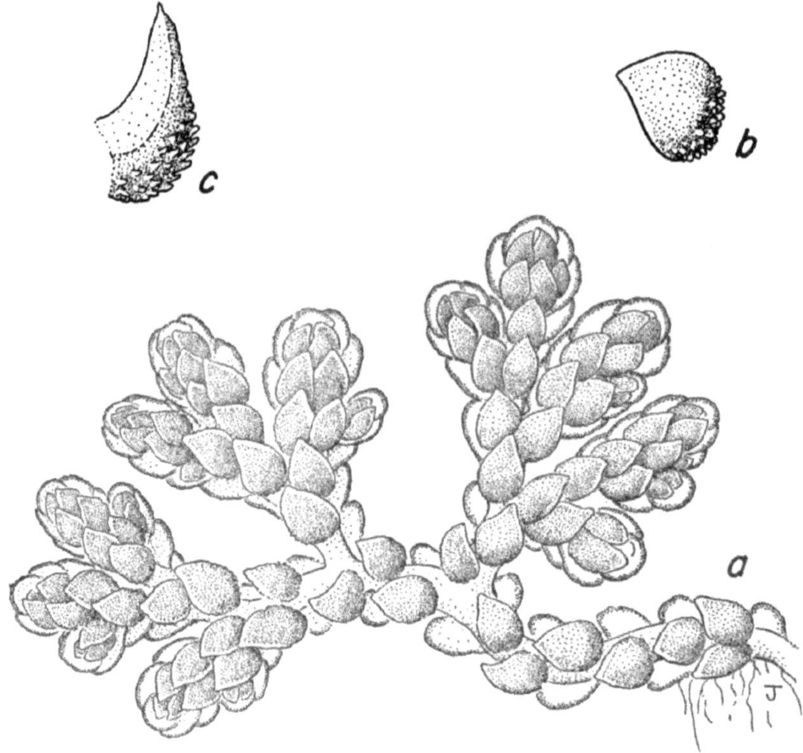

FIGURE 47. Azolla mexicana. (a) habit × 12, (b), (c) leaves enlarged.

V. **EQUISETACEAE** HORSETAIL FAMILY

Plants perennial, with widely creeping, branched, deeply subterranean rhizomes; aerial stems simple or branched, rush-like, jointed; nodes sheathed, the top of each crowned by a ring of pointed scales; branches, when present, in whorls; internodes hollow, fluted, the ridges roughened with siliceous tubercles or granules; leaves minute, scalelike, forming a sheath around the stem by the fusion of their bases, the apices deciduous or persistent; sporangia borne in compact terminal cones; spores uniform; gametophytes minute, independent, dioecious, green.

This family comprises a single living genus of about 60 species, widely distributed in wet, boggy habitats throughout the world. The largest species is found in the Amazon region of South America and is 1½ inches in diameter with a height of 6 to 12 feet. *Equisetum* is the only living genus of a vanishing race very abundant during the late Paleozoic Era; it included the giant *Calamites,* which often attained a diameter of 1 foot and a height of 60 feet.

1. EQUISETUM Horsetail

Some species bear slender, green, unbranched, jointed stems, while others have stems that are widely and finely branched and horsetail-like in appearance. They are commonly called scouring rushes, because of their silicon content, and the dried stems of some species are sometimes used as a scouring agent. The species listed below seldom reach over 3 feet in height.

The name *Equisetum* derives from the Latin, *equus* (horse) , and *seta* (bristle) , hence horsetail.

KEY TO THE SPECIES

1. Sterile and fertile stems distinct, the fertile ones unbranched, flesh-colored, succulent, soon withering; sterile stems green with numerous whorled, slender, lateral branches......................1. *E. arvense*

1. Sterile and fertile stems alike, green, persistent, simple or sometimes bearing a few lateral branches.

    2. Stem sheaths much longer than broad, dilated upward, the sheaths with 1 dark, narrow, apical band, the lowest sheaths also sometimes showing a dark basal band, the teeth early deciduous; stems grass-green throughout.................................2. *E. laevigatum*

    2. Stem sheaths about as wide as long, nearly cylindrical, at maturity ash-colored with 2 dark bands, the teeth mostly subpersistent or irregularly deciduous; stems olive-green....................3. *E. hiemale*

1. **Equisetum arvense** L., Sp. Pl. 1061. 1753. Common, Field, or Meadow Horsetail. (Figure 48.)

Fertile fronds appearing in early spring; sterile fronds usually developing from the rhizomes after the fertile shoots have died down. Fertile shoots soft pale brown in color, 4 to 10 inches tall with loose, dark-colored, 8- to 12-toothed sheaths; cones pedunculate, 1 to 2 inches long; sterile shoots green, slender, 10 to 20 inches tall, 10- to 14-furrowed, with numerous,

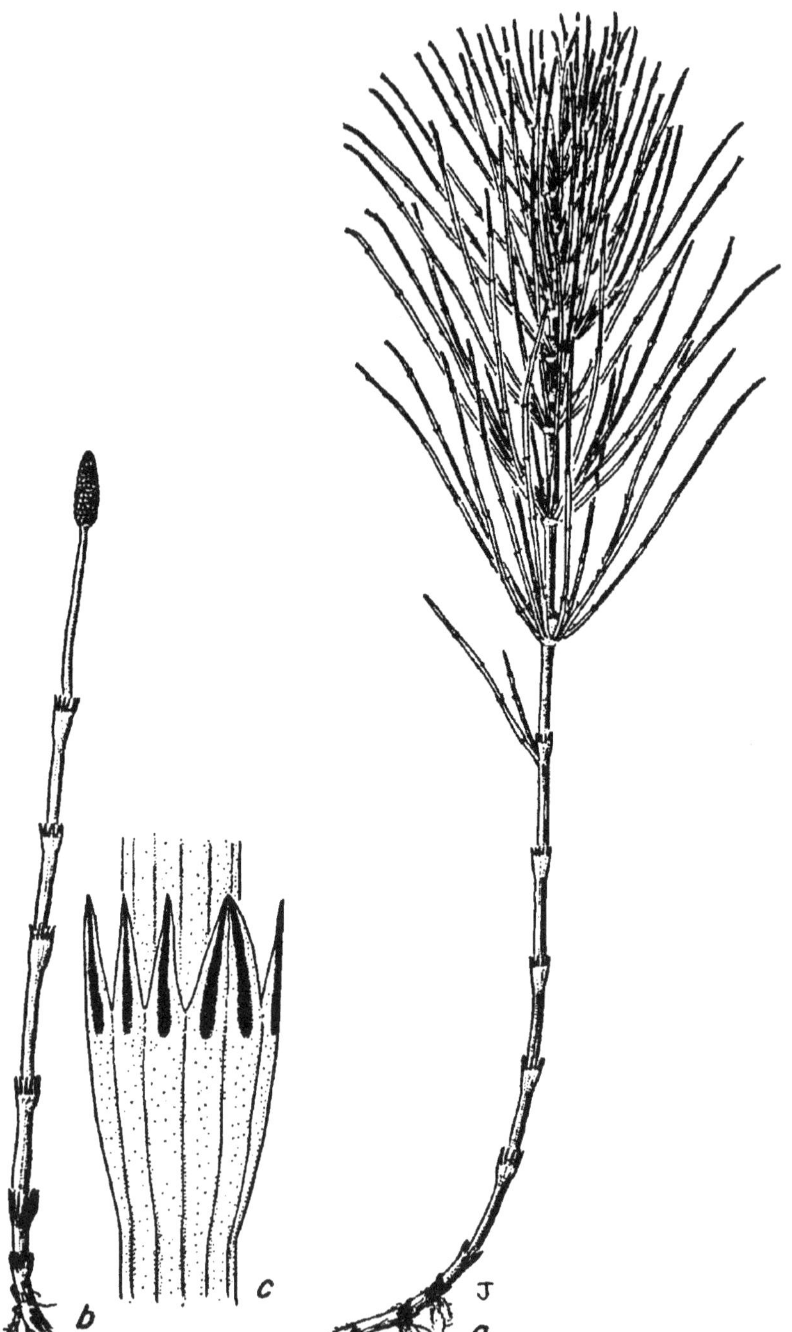

FIGURE 48. Equisetum arvense. (a) habit × ½, (b) fertile shoot showing cone × ½, (c) node of fertile shoot × 10.

verticillate, 3- to 4-angled branches having 4-toothed sheaths; rootstocks felted, often bearing tubers. Occasionally the sterile stems bear small cones in summer or fall.

This species is widely distributed throughout nearly all of the United States and Canada and southward into Mexico; Greenland; Eurasia.

New Mexico: Generally along mountain streams and irrigation ditches. Jemez, Mogollon, Santa Fe, and Las Vegas mountains; Black Range; Taos, Farmington, Albuquerque.

2. **Equisetum laevigatum** A. Br., Amer. Journ. Sci. 46: 87. 1844. SMOOTH HORSETAIL, SMOOTH or SUMMER SCOURING RUSH. (Figure 49.)

Stems 10 to 40 inches tall, 2 to 8 mm. wide, 15- to 30-grooved, simple, or rarely sparingly branched; sheaths green, longer than broad, dilated upward, the teeth mostly promptly deciduous, their bases making up the conspicuous narrow black band which appears at the apex of each sheath; occasionally a second band may be seen at the base of some of the lower sheaths; terminal cones about ½ to 1 inch long, 5 mm. wide, blunt to sharply apiculate, sessile or nearly so.

This species grows most abundantly on moist, alluvial ditch banks or in thickets and may appear as a weed in cultivated fields. It ranges from British Columbia to Ontario and southward to Mexico and Guatemala, including in the United States such states as New York, Illinois, Ohio, Missouri, Oklahoma, Texas, New Mexico, Arizona, Colorado, and California.

New Mexico: Streams and meadows at lower altitudes in the White, San Andres, Mogollon, Capitan, Jemez, Santa Fe, and Las Vegas mountains; Sangre de Cristo and Black ranges; Albuquerque, Shiprock, Rio Arriba, Taos, Ute Park, Santa Rosa, Las Cruces, Cliff, north of Ramah, Paradise Valley north of Clayton, Jornada Experimental Range.

SYNONYMY

Equisetum hyemale var. *intermedium* A. A. Eaton, Fern Bull. 10: 120. 1902.
Equisetum kansanum Schaffn., Ohio Nat. 13: 21. 1912.
Equisetum intermedium Rydb., Flora of Rocky Mts. 1053. 1917.

3. Equisetum hiemale L., Sp. Pl. 1062. 1753. SCOURING RUSH. (Figure 50.)

Stems olive-green, rather rigid, rarely branched, 20 to 40 inches tall, usually more than 8 mm. wide; stem ridges with two rows of tubercles, appearing as cross-banding on the ridges although often more or less confluent and indistinct; sheaths cylindrical, closely appressed to the stem, often split longitudinally, usually ash-colored at maturity, bearing a conspicuous basal band and an equally prominent apical band on each sheath; teeth of the sheath brown and obscurely 4-keeled, irregularly deciduous; cones ¼ to ½ inch long and strongly apiculate.

This species prefers moist, alluvial soil especially along streams and springs. Similar in its distribution to the other species, it ranges from Nova Scotia to British Columbia south to southern California and Florida; Mexico.

New Mexico: Low areas along streams in the White, Tunitcha, Santa Fe, and Las Vegas mountains; Sangre de Cristo and Black ranges; Las Cruces, Cedar Hill in San Juan County.

This species is quite variable. Presumably typical *E. hiemale* does not occur in New Mexico. Our specimens appear to be *E. hiemale* var. *elatum* (Engelm.) Morton.

SYNONYMY

Equisetum prealtum Raf., Fl. Ludovic. 13. 1817.
Equisetum robustum A. Br., Amer. Journ. Sci. 46: 88. 1843.
Equisetum laevigatum var. *elatum* Engelm., Amer. Journ. Sci. 46: 87. 1843.
Equisetum hiemale var. *robustum* (A. Br.) A. A. Eaton, Fern Bull. 11: 75, 112. 1903.
Equisetum hiemale var. *elatum* (Engelm.) Morton, Leafl. West. Bot. 6: 156. 1951.

VI. ISOËTACEAE QUILLWORT FAMILY

Aquatic or amphibious plants with fleshy, flattened stems (corms); leaves crowded, all fertile, simple and onionlike, spirally arranged atop the corm, entire, glabrous and scaleless, hollow, and divided into 4 longitudinal cavities which bear cross walls at irregular intervals; roots dichotomously branched; sporangia large, oblong, in the hollow leaf bases, divided by transverse partitions; megaspores large; microspores small, nu-

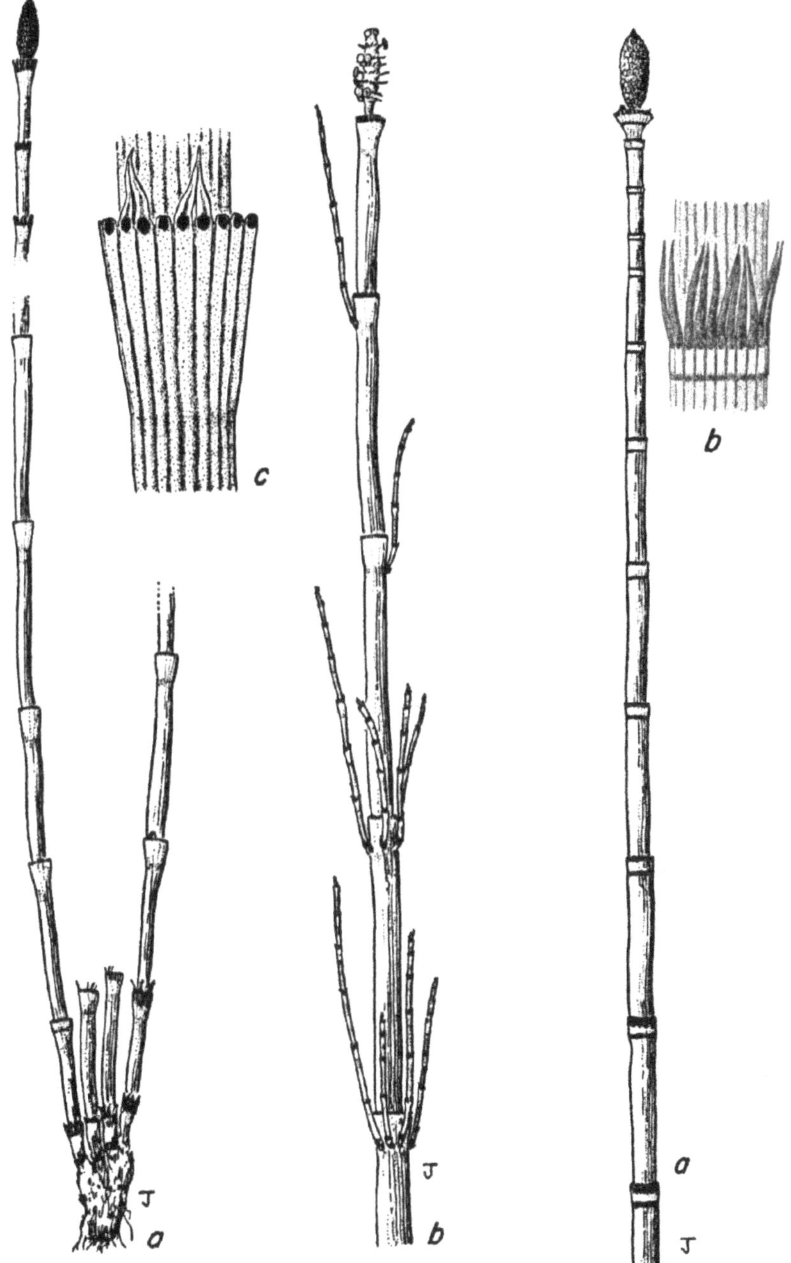

FIGURE 49. Equisetum laevigatum. (a), (b) plant showing cone × ½, (c) node showing sheath × 5.

FIGURE 50. Equisetum hiemale. (a) plant showing cone × ½, (b) node showing sheath × 5.

merous; gametophytes reduced, dioecious, borne entirely within the spore walls.

The family consists of a single genus, *Isoëtes,* comprising about 80 species distributed throughout the world but most numerous in the North Temperate Zone. The name is Greek in origin and means "equal year," apparently a reference to the persistent green leaves, that is, equal at all seasons of the year.

1. ISOËTES Quillwort

1. Isoëtes Bolanderi Engelm., Amer. Nat. 8: 214. 1874.

Corms two-lobed; leaves 2 to 10 inches tall, tapering to a fine point; ligules small, cordate; velum (a fold of leaf tissue) narrow and covering the upper end of the orbicular or oval sporangia; megaspores white or slate-blue.

This species is found in mountain ponds and lakes from British Columbia to Wyoming, Colorado, Arizona, and California. The genus name is one used by Pliny for a species of *Sedum.*

This inconspicuous plant has not been reported from the state, but its distribution in Colorado and Arizona suggests that it is to be found in New Mexico also.

VII. SELAGINELLACEAE Spikemoss Family

Plants evergreen, terrestrial, perennial, mosslike; stems slender, erect or prostrate, subdichotomously branched, with one vascular bundle; leaves very small, numerous, scalelike, simple, spirally arranged in four or more ranks, one-nerved, usually ciliate on the margins; terminal fruiting spikes comprised of fertile leaves (sporophylls) which resemble the foliage leaves and bear the microsporangia and megasporangia.

The family consists of a single living genus, *Selaginella,* the name being a diminutive of *Selago,* an ancient designation of the genus *Lycopodium,* to which it is closely related. Usually found in rocky situations in Mexico and the United States, but mostly in humid, forest soils of the tropics, although some reach the arctic.

KEY TO THE SPECIES

1. Plants forming definite rosettes, all the divisions flattened.

  2. Leaves rounded, with conspicuously whitish margins, lacking setae.
                       1. *S. lepidophylla*

  2. Leaves ovate, with acute apex, each bearing an elongated seta.
                       2. *S. pilifera*

1. Plants not forming rosettes, creeping, the divisions not strongly flattened.

    3. Stems prostrate, rooting throughout.

      4. Branches uniformly slender, elongated.

        5. Plants blue-green, leaves closely appressed giving the stems a wiry, rigid appearance, setae very short or wanting.
                       3. *S. mutica*

        5. Plants bright dark green, leaves lax and somewhat spreading, setae prominent.........................4. *S. Underwoodii*

      4. Vegetative branches very short, stout, tufted, branches and leaves upcurved and recurved, giving an appearance of dorsiventrality.

        6. Plants strongly dorsiventral, i.e., having an upper (ventral) and a lower (dorsal) surface..............5. *S. arizonica*

        6. Plants not dorsiventral, although the branches and leaves often upcurved and recurved giving an appearance of dorsiventrality, the upper and lower leaves alike.

          7. Setae very short, stiff, yellowish to whitish-yellow in color (or brownish in age)..............6. *S. Wrightii*

          7. Setae prominent, whitish-hyaline.

            8. Spikes few, arcuately ascending, the leaf setae conspicuously spinulose.....................7. *S. Sheldonii*

            8. Spikes numerous, erect, the leaf setae inconspicuously spinulose.

              9. Spikes not more than $\frac{1}{2}$ inch long, leaf setae in tufts, conspicuously irregularly wavy...8. *S. densa*

              9. Spikes more than $\frac{1}{2}$ inch long, leaf setae not tufted, straighter..............9. *S. scopulorum*

    3. Stems mostly erect and rooting only in the lower half.

            10. Plants light olive-green to bright green, cilia of leaf margins short dentiform.
                   10. *S. Weatherbiana*

            10. Plants bluish-green to gray-green, with numerous prominent cilia on the leaf margins.

> 11. Leaves whitish-marginate, lance-aciculate, evenly attenuate to a very long, stiff, yellowish-white seta........11. *S. rupincola*
>
> 11. Leaves not marginate, subulate-attenuate to an acutish apex, giving rise rather abruptly to the short, whitish-hyaline seta. 12. *S. neomexicana*

1. Selaginella lepidophylla (Hook. & Grev.) Spring, Monog. Lycopod. 2: 72. 1849. RESURRECTION PLANT.

Branches rooting chiefly toward the base; leaves closely imbricate in a very regular pattern, rounded with obtuse apex, the margins whitish, setae wanting; spikes numerous, distinctly quadrangular; sporophylls ovate, acutish in appearance differing sharply from the vegetative leaves.

During most of the year the plant is an inconspicuous brownish ball of recurved and inrolled leaves. Only after a rain do the branches unroll, forming flat, bright-green rosettes. Very slow growing.

On dry, north-facing, rocky slopes and ledges in limestone areas, it ranges from western Texas and New Mexico south to southern Sonora.

New Mexico: Magdalena and San Andres mountains; probably will be found in the Guadalupe Mountains.

2. Selaginella pilifera A. Br., Ind. Sem. Hort. Berol. Append. 1857: 20. 1857. RESURRECTION PLANT. (Figure 51.)

Habit similar to that of *S. lepidophylla* but with more slender, less rigid, and paler green stems; branches about 3 mm. wide including the lateral leaves; leaves ovate, acute, those of the ventral side of the branches larger than those of the dorsal, the midribs wide and darker green especially on the under surface, the conspicuous, long, leaf setae approximately half as long as the leaf blade; outer margin of lateral leaves strongly short-ciliate toward base.

Apparently confined to limestone, this species ranges through the mountains of western Texas and adjacent south-

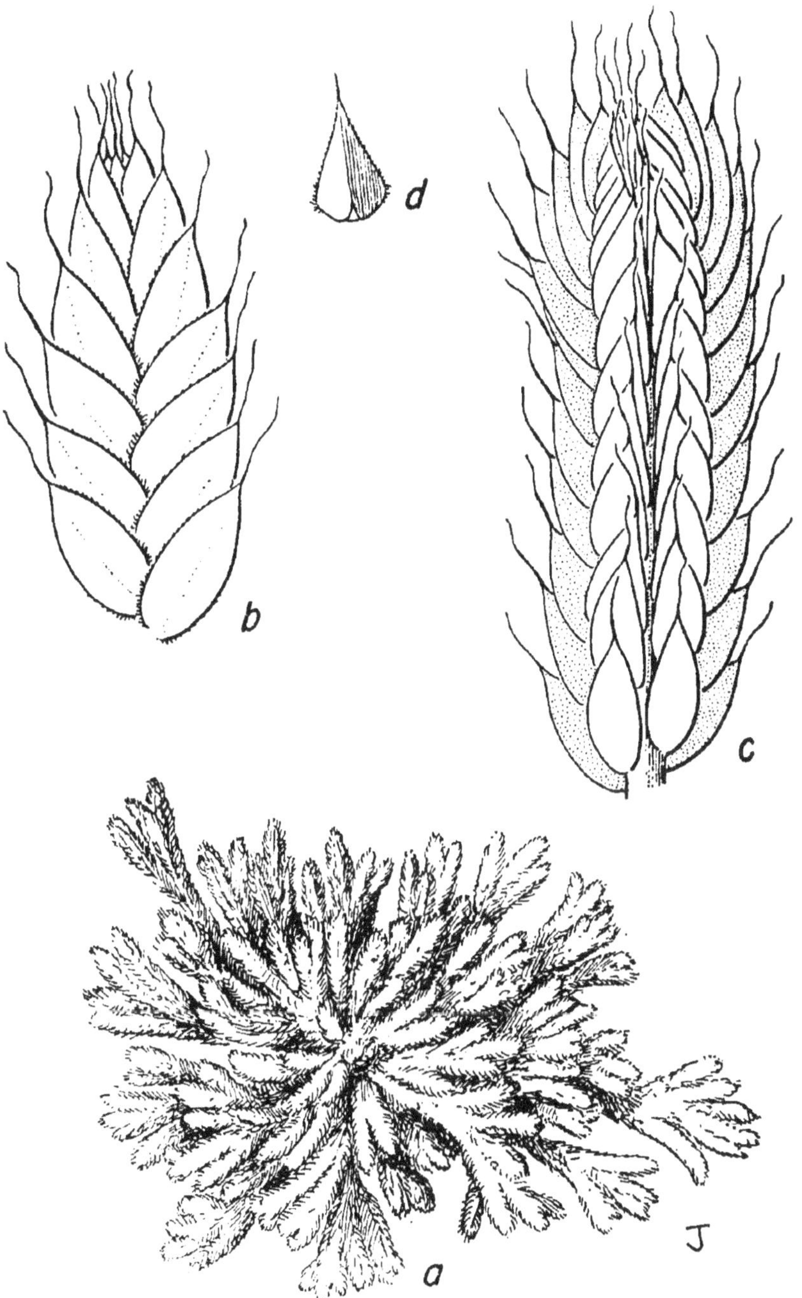

FIGURE 51. Selaginella pilifera. (a) habit × 1¼, (b) ventral view, tip of branch × 10, (c) dorsal view, tip of branch × 10, (d) sporophyll × 10.

eastern New Mexico southward to northern Sonora, Coahuila, San Luis Potosi, Nuevo Leon, and northern Tamaulipas.

New Mexico: Guadalupe Mountains.

SYNONYMY

Selaginella Pringlei Baker, Handb. Fern Allies 88. 1887.
Selaginella pilifera var. *Pringlei* (Baker) Morton, Amer. Fern Journ. 29: 15. 1939.

3. Selaginella mutica D. C. Eaton ex Underw., Bull. Torr. Bot. Club 25: 128. 1898.

Stems creeping, rather rigid, wiry, uniformly very slender, 3 to 6 inches long, divided and pinnately branched, provided with roots on many of their branches; leaves glaucescent, six-ranked, closely appressed to the stem, short-adnate at the usually rounded or truncate base, strongly convex dorsally, ovate-oblong to narrowly oblong in the different varieties, obtuse to acutish or short-mucronate, with or without short terminal setae, the margins with spreading cilia on each side; spikes scarcely thicker than the branches, quadrangular, the sporophylls broader than the leaves and pointed or even obscurely mucronate.

On damp cliffs in the mountains, especially on limestone, sandstone, and basalt, this species ranges in the montane regions of southwestern Texas to Colorado, northern and central New Mexico, northern Arizona with a single record from the south-eastern part of the state, and eastern Utah. Found in the same habitat as *S. Underwoodii* and frequently intermingled with this spikemoss in growth.

New Mexico: Organ, White, Sacramento, Magdalena, San Andres, Guadalupe, San Mateo, Nacimiento, Santa Fe, and Las Vegas mountains; mountains west of Deming; Rio Grande Canyon west of Taos; near Santa Rosa.

C. A. Weatherby (Journ. Arnold Arbor. 25: 407. 1944.) has differentiated three varieties of *S. mutica*. For the purposes of this manual it seems inadvisable to make these distinctions.

4. Selaginella Underwoodii Hieron. in Engler and Prantl, Nat. Pflanzenfam. I, 4: 714. 1901. (Figure 52.)

Plants brilliant dark green when young, stems creeping freely, branching and rooting throughout, 4 to 6 inches long;

FIGURE 52. Selaginella Underwoodii. (a) habit × 1, (b) strobili × 9, (c) leaf × 9, (d) sporophyll × 9, (e) sporophyll showing megasporangium × 13.

leaves loosely imbricate, lax and spreading, rather crowded, linear to subulate-lanceolate, the acute apex terminating in prominent hyaline setae which vary in length, the leaves bearing lateral cilia ranging from small teeth or obsolescence to well-developed and piliform; spikes rather short ($\frac{1}{5}$ to $\frac{4}{5}$ inch), the sporophylls ovate-deltoid, cordate at base, each with an apical seta much like those of the foliage leaves.

On moist cliffs and ledges ranging from southwestern Texas through western Oklahoma, New Mexico, Arizona, Colorado, and Wyoming. Often associated with *S. mutica.*

New Mexico: Organ, White, Mogollon, Bear, San Mateo, Magdalena, Sandia, Jemez, Santa Fe, and Las Vegas mountains; Sangre de Cristo and Black ranges; Ute Park; near Folsom; Brazos Canyon (northeastern Rio Arriba County); and near Reserve.

C. A. Weatherby has divided this species into typical *S. Underwoodii* and *S. Underwoodii* var. *dolichotricha,* in New Mexico, the former occurring in the northern, the latter in the southern part of the state, being found in the Black Range, the Mogollon Mountains, as well as in Arizona.

SYNONYMY

Selaginella rupestris var. *Fendleri* Underw., Bull. Torr. Bot. Club 25: 127. 1898.
Selaginella Fendleri (Underw.) Hieron., Hedwigia 39: 303. 1900.

5. **Selaginella arizonica** Maxon, Smiths. Misc. Coll. 72(5): 5. 1920.

Plants wholly prostrate, the main stems up to 8 inches long, rooting at intervals throughout, pinnately branched, the lower and middle ones twice-pinnate, the ultimate branches broadly subclavate, short, strongly dorsiventral, all the parts densely leafy; leaves unequal, crowded, in six ranks, lanceolate, short-ciliate, those of the under ranks obliquely imbricate, upcurved, clasping, those on the upper side narrower, acuminate, terminating in short, more or less reflexed, persistent or fugacious setae; leaves at first bright green, graying with age; spikes short, ascending, little differentiated in appearance from the vegetative branches, sometimes numerous; sporophylls narrowly ovate-deltoid, barely setaceous, serrate to short-ciliate.

This species is distributed from western Texas to Arizona and Sonora.

Although no specimen has been reported from New Mexico, its occurrence in western Texas and in eastern Arizona suggests that it is to be found in New Mexico.

6. Selaginella Wrightii Hieron., Hedwigia 39: 298. 1900.

Stems clustered, creeping, much-branched, frequently crowded, 2½ to 4 inches long, very freely rooting, and giving an appearance of dorsiventrality; leaves crowded, appressed, longer and narrower than in *S. Sheldonii,* tending to be laterally arranged, rather firm, papery, each having the apex tipped with a short, stiff, brownish to yellowish seta; each leaf bears long cilia on each side; spikes erect (about twice as long as in *S. Sheldonii*), commonly produced in great abundance, the sporophylls long, narrow. In appearance this species resembles *S. densa.*

Apparently growing only on limestone, carpeting the ground under sheltering rocks or on ledges on north-facing cliffs, it ranges from the Edwards Plateau in Texas westward to southeastern New Mexico, El Paso, and to San Luis Potosi, and possibly to Puebla.

New Mexico: Sacramento and Guadalupe mountains.

7. Selaginella Sheldonii Maxon, Proc. Biol. Soc. Wash. 31: 171. 1918.

Plants prostrate, the sterile branches upcurved and recurved, the main stems up to 5 inches long, rooting throughout, densely pinnately branched, the lower branches often spreading, mostly bipinnate; stems, branches, and minor divisions all densely leafy, the leaves tending to be laterally spreading and mostly curving upward, giving a definite dorsiventral appearance; leaves crowded, imbricate, all grayish-green, subulate to lance-subulate, acute at the apex, each terminating in a slender elongate, persistent, white seta, each leaf with widely oblique, short cilia on both sides; spikes few, arcuately ascending, the sporophylls ovate to narrowly deltoid-ovate, long-acuminate.

This species does not necessarily grow on rocks and usually

is found on flat areas above limestone or igneous cliffs; it ranges from southwestern Oklahoma and central and western Texas to New Mexico.

New Mexico: Dona Ana Mountains; vicinity of Las Vegas; Watrous; vicinity of Santa Fe; mountains of northern New Mexico; Pine Canyon in Eddy County.

8. Selaginella densa Rydb., Mems. N. Y. Bot. Gard. 1: 7. 1900. (Figure 53.)

Stems densely tufted, rooting throughout, in color usually yellowish-green; sterile branches very short, crowded, and usually recurved and upcurved, giving a distinct appearance of dorsiventrality; leaves densely crowded and many-ranked, linear, or in age almost needle-shaped, thickened, ciliate on the margins, each leaf abruptly attenuate into a long, conspicuously irregularly wavy seta; spikes erect, quadrangular, not more than ½ inch long but usually longer than the vegetative branches; sporophylls imbricate, triangular-ovate, ciliate on the margins from base to seta, the setae about half the length of those of the leaves.

Selaginella densa is closely related to *S. scopulorum*. However, *S. densa* is readily recognized by the conspicuous tufts of very long, slender white setae at the ends of the branches. In *S. scopulorum* the terminal setae are not only shorter, stiffer, and more nearly straight, but are whitish-hyaline from a plainly yellowish base, and they are never aggregated in tufts, as in *S. densa*. The blades of the foliage leaves are different in the two species, those of *S. densa* being obtuse and terminating abruptly in a long, filiform, irregularly wavy and somewhat spinulose seta, while those of *S. scopulorum* are less obtuse, tapering slightly to the seta proper from a thick, distinctly yellow base. The sporophylls of *S. densa*, moreover, are conspicuously long-ciliate, with oblique hairs; in *S. scopulorum* the sporophyll cilia are very much shorter, less oblique, and much less numerous or even lacking.

Common on exposed hillsides, in New Mexico especially at high altitudes. A characteristic species of the Rocky Mountains, it ranges from British Columbia, Washington, and Idaho

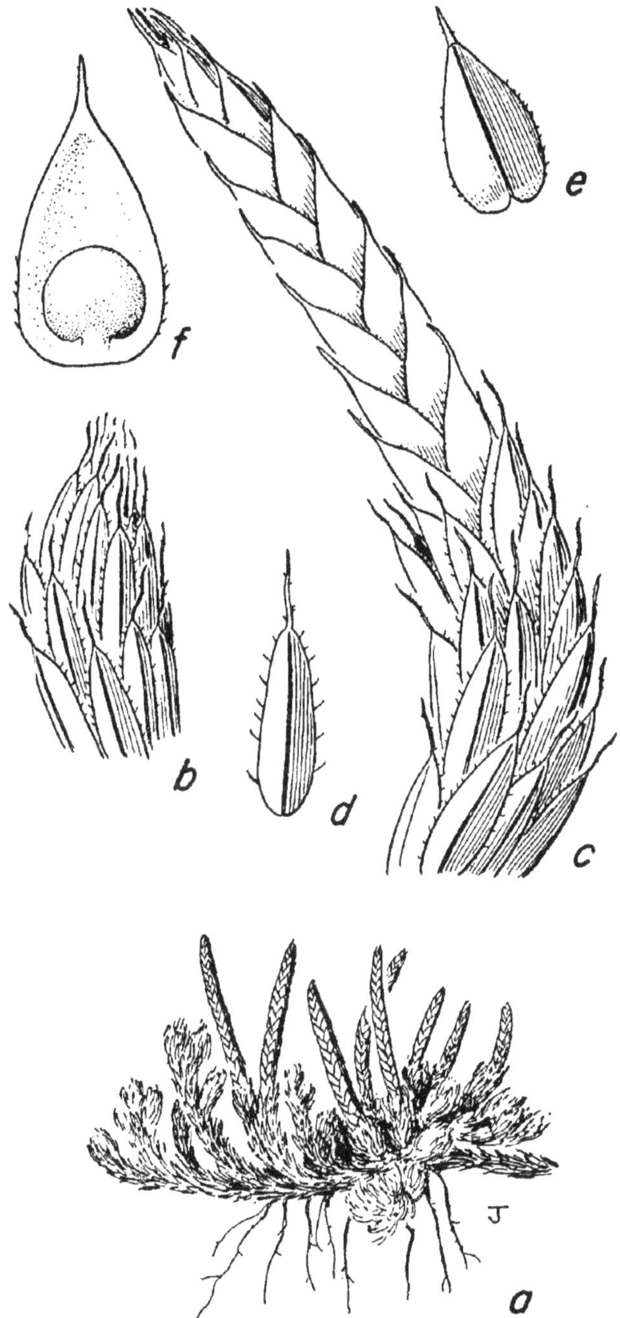

FIGURE 53. Selaginella densa. (a) habit × 1½, (b) tip of branch × 10, (c) strobilus × 10, (d) leaf × 10, (e) sporophyll × 10, (f) sporophyll showing megasporangium × 15.

east to Alberta and southward through Montana, South Dakota, Colorado and Utah, to New Mexico and Arizona.

New Mexico: Sangre de Cristo and Black ranges, Hillsboro Peak, Mt. Taylor, Jemez, Sandia, and Las Vegas mountains; Santa Rosa.

9. **Selaginella scopulorum** Maxon, Amer. Fern Journ. 11(2): 36. 1921.

Stems prostrate, short-creeping, 1¼ to 2½ inches long, pinnately branched, subcespitose, forming large mats; branches numerous, close, the sterile ones mostly ¼ to ¾ inch long, ascending and recurved, giving a definite dorsiventral appearance, simple or with several very short, oblique divisions; leaves appressed-imbricate, papery, subglaucous, lance-subulate to narrowly ovate; setae on both leaves and sporophylls long, stiff, whitish-hyaline from a yellowish base; cilia on both short, those on the sporophyll margins few or none and located toward the base of the sporophyll; spikes numerous, ½ to 2 inches long, slender, quadrangular, erect; sporophylls leathery, broadly ovate, long-acuminate (setae included).

This species ranges through British Columbia, Washington, Oregon, Montana, Wyoming, Colorado, and New Mexico.

New Mexico: Mt. Taylor, Lake Peak, Black Range, Santa Rosa.

10. **Selaginella Weatherbiana** Tryon, Amer. Fern Journ. 40(1): 69. 1950.

Plants 2 to 6 inches long; stems of two kinds: one prostrate, creeping, subterranean, sparingly branched and sparingly rooted throughout; the other erect, aerial, rooting only at the base or rarely decumbent at the base and rooting in the basal half, abundantly branched especially above the base, the pinnately divided branches becoming bipinnate; leaves of the prostrate stems oblong-ovate, very long-adnate to the stem, whitish or pale whitish-green, the marginal cilia usually numerous, ascending or spreading, leaf setae short to long (our specimens bearing rather long setae); vegetative leaves of the erect stems ascending, six-ranked, long-adnate, wholly concealing the stem, longer than those on the prostrate stems, subulate-linear, light olive-green to bright green, occasionally lightly glaucous, cilia of the leaf margins short, few to numerous, dentiform, more abundant and spreading toward the base, fewer and ascending above; leaf setae long, conspicuous; sporophylls narrowly deltoid-ovate, slightly biauriculate, the marginal cilia numerous and not different in length from those on the vegetative leaves of the aerial stems.

This species ranges through Colorado and northern New Mexico.

New Mexico: Santa Fe and Las Vegas mountains; Ute Park.

11. **Selaginella rupincola** Underw., Bull. Torr. Bot. Club 25: 129. 1898. (Figure 54.)

Stems suberect to nearly erect and ascendingly branched, somewhat flexuous, 3 to 8 inches long, rooting chiefly from near the base, pinnately branched, the secondary branches mostly very short, shoots symmetrical and equally clothed on all sides by appressed leaves; leaves closely imbricate, spreading only near the stem tips, abruptly adnate to the stem, bluish to grayish-green, often whitish-marginate, narrowly lanceolate, tapering to very long, stiff setae which give the appearance of a conspicuous whitish tuft at the ends of the sterile shoots, leaf margins with numerous cilia on each side; spikes ½ inch long or less, borne laterally on the branches, scarcely quadrangular, the sporophylls strongly resembling the leaves except that their cilia are not so conspicuous.

Apparently confined to igneous rocks, especially dry granite ledges or crevices in rugged outcroppings of basalt, this species ranges from western Texas through southern New Mexico and southern Arizona southward into Mexico along the western Sierra Madre to Durango and Guanajuato.

New Mexico: Organ, San Luis, and Burro mountains; Dog Spring, Guadalupe Canyon (Hidalgo County).

12. **Selaginella neomexicana** Maxon, Smiths. Misc. Coll. 72(5): 2. 1920. (Figure 55.)

Plants bluish-green to gray-green, 4 to 8 inches long, rooting only in the extreme lower portion, freely branching, all the

FIGURE 54. Selaginella rupincola. (a) habit × 1½, (b) leaf × 15. (c) strobilus × 10, (d) sporophyll × 10, (e) sporophyll showing microsporangium × 15.

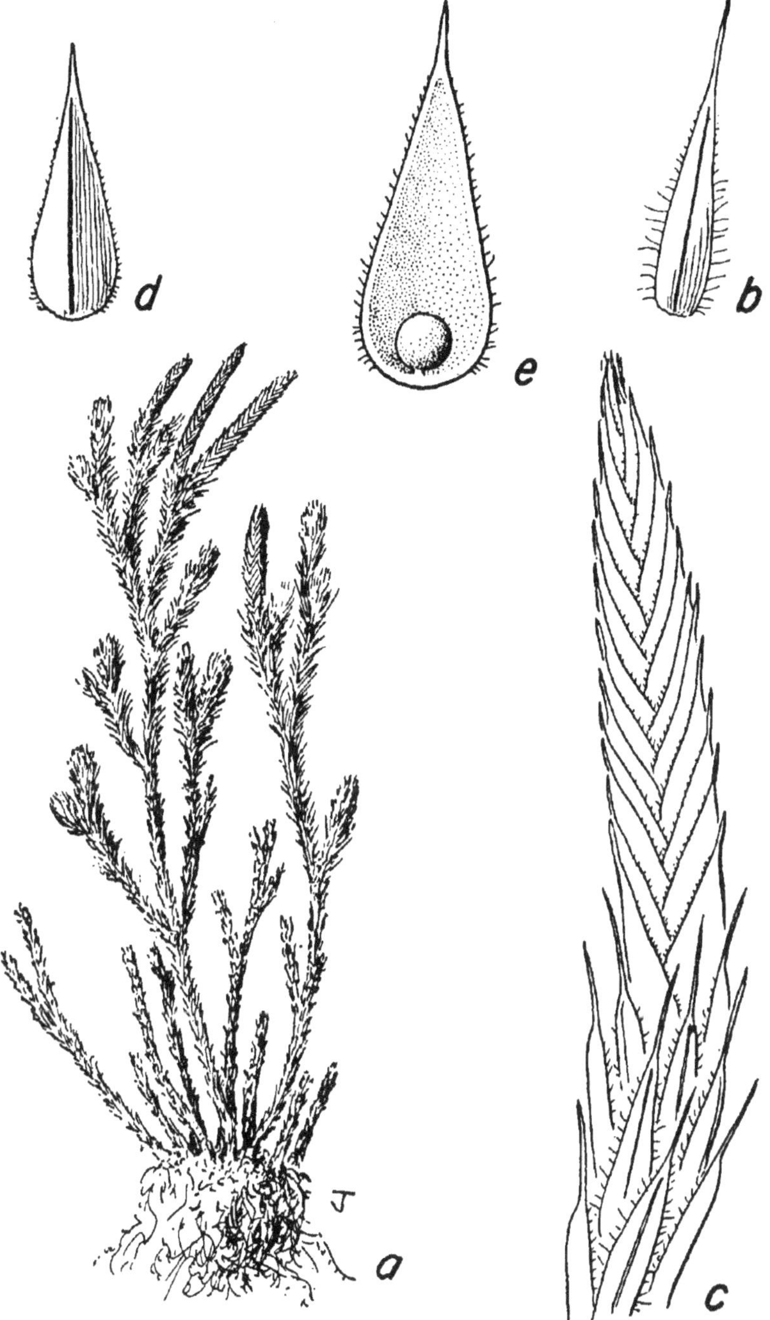

FIGURE 55. Selaginella neomexicana. (a) habit × 1½, (b) leaf × 15, (c) strobilus × 11, (d) sporophyll × 11, (e) sporophyll showing abortive megasporangium × 17.

branches erect or ascending, several times pinnate; leaves abruptly adnate to the stem, subulate-attenuate to an acute apex, not marginate, with a deep, narrow median groove, and giving rise rather abruptly to the short, whitish-hyaline setae; leaves with numerous piliform cilia on each side; spikes numerous, terminating the main branches, ¼ to ¾ inch long, somewhat curved, sharply quadrangular; megasporangia abortive.

This species ranges through western Texas and has been found in southern New Mexico and southern Arizona (a single collection).

New Mexico: Modoc in the Organ Mountains at 5,500 feet.

GLOSSARY

Aciculate, acicular. Slenderly needle-shaped.

Acuminate. Gradually tapering to apex.

Acute. Terminating in a sharp or well-defined angle.

Adnate. Grown together, as leaflets attached to rachis.

Adventitious. Roots arising in an unusual position, as from a rhizome or leaf.

Aerial. Parts above ground or out of water.

Alluvial. Pertaining to a deposit of earth, sand, or other material, made by the ordinary mechanical action of running water.

Alternate. Applied to leaves when not opposite or whorled on the rachis or rachilla, but borne singly at regular intervals at different levels.

Alternation of generations. In successive generations of sexual and asexual plants.

Amphibious. Capable of growing in both water and soil.

Anastomosing. Connecting by cross-veins and forming a network.

Antheridium (pl. *antheridia*). The male sexual organ of ferns, etc., analogous to the anther in flowering plants.

Apex (pl. *apices*, adj. *apical*). Tip of an organ; relating to the apex or tip.

Apiculate. With a short, abrupt terminal point.

Apogamous. Developing without fertilization.

Appressed. Lying flat against another part.

Aquatic. Growing submerged or mostly submerged in water.

Arachnoid. Cobwebby, bearing fine, weak, tangled hairs.

Archegonium (pl. *archegonia*). The female sexual organ of ferns, containing the egg cells.

Arcuate (adv. *arcuately*). Moderately curved; arching.

Articulate. Jointed.

Asymmetrical. Irregular.

Attenuate. Slenderly tapering; gradually becoming very narrow or slender.

Auriculate, auricled. With earlike basal appendages.

Axil. The inner angle where one organ is united with another, especially the angle between leaf and stem.

Axis (of the stem). The central part of a longitudinal support on which organs or parts are arranged.

Base. Lower portion of blade or leaf.

Bipinnate. Twice-pinnate, the segments along the rachis being again pinnate.

Bipinnatifid. Twice-pinnatifid, the main segments again pinnatifid, none of the segments completely formed into separate leaflets.

Blade. The expanded portion of a leaf or frond.

Bract. A reduced or modified leaf.

Calamites. A fossil member of the Equisetales.

Calcareous. Having a large amount of limestone ($CaCO_3$).

Canescent. Gray or hoary, usually referring to pubescence.

Castaneous. Chestnut-colored, i.e., reddish-brown.

Cespitose. Growing in tufts.

Chaffy. Bearing dry, membranaceous scales.

Chartaceous. Rather stiff, papery.

Cilium (pl. *cilia*, adj. *ciliate*). A marginal hair.

Circinate. Coiled into a circle or partially so; the usual manner in which a fern leaf is formed before expanding (see vernation).

Clavate. Club-shaped.

Concave. Hollow and curved or rounded; said of the interior of a curved surface or line.

Concolorous. Of uniform color.

Cone. A strobilus; the more or less conic, bracted, fruiting structure of *Equisetum* and related plants.

Confluent. Passing gradually into one another, as confluent varieties.

Cordate. Heart-shaped.

Cordaites. Fossilized seed-ferns, actually gymnosperms.

Cordlike. Resembling cord or twine.

Coriaceous. Thick and leathery in texture.

Corm. The underground bulblike, fleshy, solid base of a stem.

Corymb. A flat-topped or convex open flower (or comparable structure) cluster.

Creeping. With stems running on or just below the surface of the ground and rooting at the nodes.

Crenate. The margin with rounded teeth, therefore scalloped.

Crustaceous. Of hard and brittle texture.

Cutinized. Having a waxy covering, as the epidermis of leaves.

Cycads. A group of tropical to subtropical gymnosperms somewhat resembling ferns.

Deciduous. Falling, as leaves or other plant parts, usually rather early, in contrast to persistent.

Decompound. Several times divided, the main divisions again being compound.

Decumbent. Prostrate with the apex ascending.

Deltoid. Shaped like the Greek letter $\triangle$.

Dentate. Margin sharp-toothed, the teeth directed outward.

Denticulate. Diminutive of dentate, i.e., having very small teeth.

Dentiform. Toothlike.

Desiccated. Dried out.

Dichotomous. Forking regularly by pairs.

Dimorphic. Having two forms.

Dioecious. Having the two sexes on different individual plants.

Diploid. The double number of chromosomes, as found in the sporophyte of ferns.

Dissected. Deeply and usually finely cut or divided, as are many leaves.

Divaricate. Widely spreading.

Dorsal. Referring to the back or outer surface of an organ; in ferns the under side of a leaf.

Dorsiventral. Having an upper (ventral) and a lower (dorsal) surface.

Elliptical. Widest in the center and longer than oval, usually about twice as long as wide.

Embryo. The young plant of the next generation produced in the archegonium.

Entire. Not toothed or lobed.

Epiphyte (adj. *epiphytic*). A plant growing attached to another plant but not parasitic.

Erose. Irregularly indented as if gnawed.

False indusium. A protective covering over the sporangia, usually formed by the recurved margin of the leaf.

Fasciculate. Bearing close bundles or clusters.

Felted. Having the soft texture of velvet.

Fertile. Portion of plant bearing spores.

Fibrous. Having or resembling fibers, as fibrous roots; much branched.

Filamentous. Resembling threads.

Filiform. Threadlike or needlelike.

Fimbriate. Fringed, having elongate, slender processes on the margin.

Flaccid. Very lax and weak, not at all rigid.

Flexuous. Bent or curved alternately in opposite directions, zigzag.

Frond. A fern leaf.

Fugacious. Falling or fading very early.

Fulvous-tomentose. Tawny, dull yellow.

Gametophyte. The sexual generation of a plant, as the prothallium of ferns, contrasted with the much larger asexual generation or sporophyte.

Glabrate. Becoming glabrous.

Glabrous. Without hairs, smooth.

Glandular. With glands; if applied to hairs, then bearing glandular, knoblike structures on the ends.

Glaucous. Covered or whitened with a bloom.

Glaucescent. Somewhat glaucous or becoming glaucous.

Globose, globular. Spherical or nearly so.

Glochid (pl. *glochidia*). A hair or a prickle with hooklike projections.

Habit. The general appearance of a plant.

Habitat. The kind of locality in which a plant grows, as woods, meadows, etc.

Haploid. Having half of the diploid (somatic) number of chromosomes, as in the germ cells after the reduction division; the number of chromosomes in the gametophytic generation.

Herbaceous. Of the texture of ordinary leaves, fairly thin.

Hispid. Roughly hairy or bristly.

Hoary. Grayish-white in appearance.

Hyaline. Thin and semitransparent.

Imbricate. Overlapping by the edge in regular succession, like shingles.

Incised. Cut sharply, deeply, and usually irregularly, as a leaf margin.

Indusium. The covering (often shield-shaped) over or around the sporangia. May be present only on the young leaf or absent altogether. See also false indusium.

Inferior. Below, usually applied to a structure below another. Applied to the indusium, it means borne below and surrounding the sporangia.

Internode. The portion between two successive nodes of a stem.

Keel. A central, dorsal ridge, like the keel of a boat.

Lacerate. With margins irregularly cut or cleft, as if torn.

Laciniate. Incised, with narrow lobes, as if slashed.

Lance-oblong. Between lance-shaped and oblong.

Lance-ovate. Between lance-shaped and egg-shaped.

Lanceolate. Widest below the middle, narrow and tapering to the apex.

Ligule. A projection from the summit of the leaf of the stem (in *Isoëtes*).

Linear. Narrow and of nearly uniform width.

Linear-subulate. Narrowly awl-shaped.

Lobed. Divided into or bearing rounded segments.

Lunate. Of the shape of a half-moon or crescent.

Massulae. The mass in which the microspores are aggregated in *Azolla*.

Median. At or pertaining to the middle.

Megasporangium (pl. *megasporangia*). The case bearing or containing the large spores (megaspores).

Megaspore. The large spore (female spore).

Membranaceous. Thin, pliable, and more or less translucent.

Microsporangia. Cases bearing the small spores (microspores).

Microspore. Small spore (male spore).

Midrib, midvein. The central nerve, rib, or vein of a leaf or similar structure.

Monoecious. Having male and female parts on the same individual plant.

Mucronate. Shortly and abruptly pointed.

Multiciliate. Bearing numerous cilia or long hairs.

Multicipital. Having many stems (caudices) in a clump.
Mycorrhiza. Enlarged roots infected with fungus strands.

Nectary. Any place or organ where nectar is secreted.
Node. The more or less swollen place on a stem at which a leaf is borne.

Oblanceolate. Like lanceolate but attached at the narrower end, wider above the middle.
Oblique. Slanting.
Oblong. Two or three times longer than broad with somewhat parallel sides.
Obovate. Inverted ovate, attached at the narrower end.
Obtuse. Apex rounded or blunt.
Orbicular. Of circular outline.
Ovate. Egg-shaped; having an outline like that of an egg, with the broader end basal.
Ovoid. Egg-shaped.

Palmate. Lobed or veined outwardly from the base, like the fingers of a hand.
Panicle. A loose, irregularly compound inflorescence with pedicellate flowers, such as a branched raceme or corymb.
Paniculate. Bearing the fruiting units on branching stalks from the main rachis.
Papillose. Covered with minute bumps or nipple-shaped protuberances.
Pectinate. Resembling a comb, having narrow, closely set teeth or divisions.
Pedicel (adj. *pedicellate, pedicelled*). The support of a single flower or comparable structure.
Peduncle. A primary stalk supporting either a cluster or a solitary flower or comparable structure.
Pedunculate. Borne upon a peduncle.
Peltate. Attached by a central stalk, somewhat like an umbrella or mushroom.
Pendant. Hanging, drooping.
Pentagonal. Five-angled.
Persistent. Long-continuous, remaining long-attached.
Petioled, petiolate. Bearing a basal stalk on the leaf.
Petiolulate. Bearing a basal stalk on a leaflet or pinnule.
Pilose. With long, soft, spreading hairs.
Pinna (pl. *pinnae*). The primary division of a pinnately compound leaf.
Pinnate. Once-compound, with the segments or leaflets arranged along an elongated rachis.
Pinnatifid. Deeply cleft along a central rachis but the clefts not extending to the rachis.
Pinnule. The ultimate division or segment of a compound pinna; one of the pinnately arranged divisions of a pinna.

Prothallium (pl. *prothallia*). The small structure representing the gametophytic generation in ferns, etc., resulting from germination of a spore and producing the sex organs.

Puberulent. With very short, fine, soft hairs.

Pubescent (n. *pubescence*). Hairy (often restricted to soft, short hairs).

Raceme. A simple inflorescence of pedicelled flowers or comparable structures upon a more or less elongated axis.

Rachilla. A little rachis; a secondary rachis.

Rachis. The main axis of a fern leaf on which the pinnae are borne.

Ranked. Position of leaves; 2-ranked means leaves arranged in two rows along the stem.

Reflexed margin. Margin of leaf turned under toward the midrib.

Reniform. Kidney-shaped.

Revolute. Margins curled back on the lower leaf surface.

Rhizome. A rootstock or prostrate stem, on or just below the ground surface, rooting at the nodes and producing buds.

Rhomboid. Diamond-shaped, attached at one angle.

Rotund. Rounded or roundish in outline.

Scabrous. Rough to the touch.

Scale. In ferns, an epidermal outgrowth, usually thin, dry, and not green.

Segment. One of the parts of the leaf or other like organ.

Septate. Having partitions; as used here, having transverse partitions.

Serrate. Sharp-toothed, with teeth directed forward or toward the apex of the structure.

Serrulate. Diminutive of serrate, i.e., with finer teeth.

Sessile. Without a stalk at the base.

Seta (pl. *setae*, adj. *setaceous*). A bristle.

Sheath. The collarlike structure at the base of the joints in *Equisetum*.

Siliceous. Containing silicon.

Sinuate. Having a strongly wavy margin.

Sinus. An indentation or recess between two lobes.

Sorus (pl. *sori*). A cluster, applied to the fruit dots (sporangia) of ferns.

Spike (adj. *spicate*). An unbranched inflorescence having the units sessile on a central rachis.

Spinulose. Having short spines or spinelike processes.

Sporangium (pl. *sporangia*). The spore-bearing case in ferns.

Spore. A reproductive cell, especially of ferns and other non-flowering plants, which produces the gametophyte.

Sporocarp. The case containing sporangia and spores; usually found in water ferns (*Marsilea*, etc.).

Sporophyll. The spore-bearing leaf in ferns, often much modified.

Sporophyte. The larger, asexual or diploid generation in ferns, etc.

Stellate. Star-shaped, applied mostly to hairs with several radiating arms.

Sterile. Not fertile, as branches or shoots not bearing sori (in ferns).

Stipe. The stalk (or petiole) of a fern leaf or frond.

Stipule. A small leaflike or bractlike structure at the base of a leaf or leaflet.

Strobilus (pl. *strobili*). A cluster of closely crowded sporophylls having the appearance of a cone.

Sub- (prefix). Somewhat, nearly, slightly.

Subacute. Nearly acute.

Subcoriaceous. Approaching a leathery condition.

Suberect. Nearly erect but somewhat angled in position.

Subflexuous. Somewhat flexuous.

Submarginal. Arising just inside the margin.

Subquadrate. Nearly square in outline.

Subternate. Nearly ternate.

Subtripinnate. Nearly 3-pinnate, the last division not always complete.

Subulate. Very narrowly triangular, awl-shaped.

Subulate-attenuate. Slender and narrowly triangular.

Superior. Above or over some other part or organ.

Tawny. Of a dull yellowish-brown color.

Terete. Cylindric, with a circular cross section, not angled.

Ternate. Arranged in threes, as with branches of the frond.

Terrestrial. Plants rooted in ground, not aquatic.

Thallus (pl. *thalli*). A vegetative body without differentiation into stem and leaf.

Tomentum (adj. *tomentose*). A covering of soft, matted hairs.

Tortuous. Twisted or bent in different directions.

Triparted. Thrice-divided.

Tripinnate. 3-times pinnate.

Tripinnatifid. Thrice-pinnatifid.

Truncate. Cut off abruptly at base or apex, not rounded.

Tuber. A thickened underground stem, bearing buds and serving for storage of reserve food.

Tubercle. A small knoblike projection or protuberance.

Tufted. Having several to many structures arising close together.

Turgid. Swollen or distended.

Ultimate segment. The last or smallest division of a leaf.

Undulate. With a wavy margin or surface.

Veins. Strands of vascular tissue, especially if branched, in a leaf or leaflike organ.

Velum. A fold of membranaceous tissue (indusium) partly enclosing the sporangium in *Isoëtes*.

Ventral. Referring to the inner or upper face of a leaf or other organ.

Vernation. The arrangement of leaves in the bud, best seen as the young leaves emerge (see *circinate*).

Verticillate. Having more than two structures attached in a whorl or circle around the stem or rachis at the same general place such as a node.

Villous. Pubescent, with long, soft, weak, slightly wavy, but not matted hairs.

Woolly. Clothed with long and tortuous or matted hairs.

Xerophytic. Adapted to dry areas.

Zygote. The cell resulting from the fusion of egg and sperm.

INDEX

Pages in *italics* are principal references.

* References to a text figure.